Seattle
Cityscape

1962 · UNIVERSITY OF WASHINGTON PRESS · SEATTLE

Seattle
Cityscape

BY VICTOR STEINBRUECK

SECOND PRINTING, 1963

Twenty minutes from the city is the wilderness that was Seattle and has always been close to its heart. One of many nearby natural or rural areas readily accessible to the city dweller and as yet unexploited is Raging River, just east of the little town of Issaquah at the foot of the Cascade Range. Nearness to the woods and mountains is one of Seattle's most attractive qualities.

Lake Washington Boulevard is part of the
extensive and beautiful boulevard system
through which one can become acquainted
with the city and its surroundings. Wooded
Seward Park on its peninsula projecting
into the lake appears in the distance, with
Mercer Island floating to the east. Beyond
each bend, other views and surprises are
waiting.

Broad, dramatic panoramas of Lake Washington, Mercer Island, Seward Park, and Mount Rainier are enjoyed from higher vantage points such as Thirtieth Avenue South and South Dearborn Street. The ever changing effects of sky and water add to the pleasure, and snow-covered Mount Rainier is an eloquent reminder of the unconquered surrounding wilderness. The first Floating Bridge has been an impressive man-made landmark since it was built in 1940.

Madrona Beach is one of many public bathing beaches that are part of the city parks and available to all. Distant Mount Baker and the Cascade Range are visible beyond the foothills arising from the lake. The bathing beaches are centers of summer activities and seem unusually quiet during other seasons. However, this off-season solitude may make them more attractive to the casual visitor.

Leschi district viewed from the Floating Bridge is a typical scene of residences and apartments fringing the lake. Changing from an area of cottages to multiple residences because of favorable zoning and property values, the waterfront has become relatively crowded. Each apartment has sought to reach farther into the lake than its predecessors. Private docks are common, and almost no waterfront resident is without his boat.

Twisting, colorful madrona trees rising on the bluff along Magnolia Boulevard are characteristic of the Puget Sound country. The boulevard, bordering a fine middle-class residential area, looks out upon Elliott Bay, the great salt-water harbor and sea entrance that made maritime development possible. Shipping and boating activities are constantly evident. Beyond are man-made Harbor Island and West Seattle, and, to the west, the islands of Vashon and Bainbridge. Here has been unfolded much of the story of Seattle.

Driving along Queen Anne Boulevard provides another experience in motion that helps one to know the city. The panoramic view progresses from the water and distant mountains to the rectangular patterns of the central business district. Contrasting size and scale relationships produce varying textures from nearby foliage and buildings to distant skylines of West Seattle and Beacon Hill, separated by industrial Harbor Island and the Duwamish Waterway. The decorative retaining wall at Eighth Avenue West was designed by architect W. R. B. Willcox in 1912.

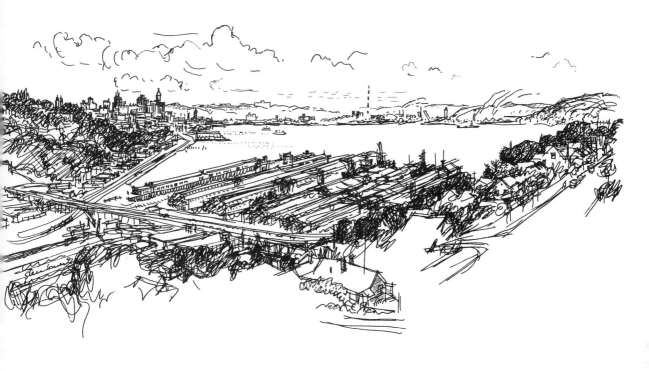

The linear pattern of the navy piers at
Smith's Cove contrasts with the downtown
skyline and distant borders of Elliott Bay
as seen from the Magnolia School play-
field. Several architectural landmarks are
visible in the downtown skyline. Smith
Tower is the most prominent and is most
often associated with Seattle as a symbol
and landmark. All of Elliott Bay is visible,
from Duwamish Head at the extreme right
to the many waterfront piers. One hundred and ten years of growth have changed
this scene from complete wilderness to one
of the world's beautiful metropolitan areas.

Capitol Hill looks out to the west over landlocked Lake Union toward Queen Anne Hill and the Aurora Bridge (actually named the George Washington Memorial Bridge) and a changing scene of industrial, commercial, and residential activity. The many marinas and boat yards reflect the involvement of Seattleites in boating of all kinds. Houseboat colonies are located in several areas along the shores. Planners hope for increased public use of the shorelands of Lake Union, which links Lake Washington and Puget Sound by means of the Lake Washington Ship Canal and the Hiram M. Chittenden Locks. Aurora Bridge has become a familiar landmark, and while not thrilling in concept it is not without grace, especially when contrasted with more recent highway structures. Eastlake district in the foreground is progressing from a generally mediocre residential community to one of apartments and small commercial businesses and offices.

The "Counterbalance" of Queen Anne Avenue North drops rapidly into the bay, opening up a distant floating world where space, sky, mountains, and water are a continual source of surprise and delight. This is a vista and a panorama familiar to all Seattleites. The "Counterbalance" was named for the old street car system of cables under the street which were hooked onto the cars to make the steep ascent possible.

Looking down Seneca Street and the other streets tilted steeply into the central business district presents a framed view of maritime activity in Elliott Bay. Many downtown workers have solved the transportation problem by eliminating it. They live on First Hill and walk to work, enjoying the view and profiting by the exercise. The new freeway, by forming a barrier between downtown and its uphill bedroom, tends to restrict this kind of development while rigidly defining the districts.

Victor Steinbrueck

Seen from west of the bay at a small lookout park on the tip of Duwamish Head, the central business district of Seattle provides a thrilling panorama by day and by night. Familiar landmarks assert themselves in the jeweled skyline. Still young in years, the city stands on the threshold of a whole new era. With an unsurpassed location and magnificent harbor, its true character and destiny will be formed by its geographical location and natural setting. Its prosperity during the formative years was based on the huge stands of virgin timber that reached down to the shores of Puget Sound. Sawmills filled ships that sailed everywhere over the globe. Fishing in nearby waters and those of Alaska was another major economic support. The second World War brought great increase in employment at Boeing and other defense industries. Today Seattle faces a future of continued change as old economic foundations disappear and new ones take their place. Progress is changing its character and image. Whatever the final outcome, it seems certain that Seattle will become one of the great cities of the world, and the years just ahead should be the most exciting in its colorful history.

Not far from this spot on Alki Beach is a marker commemorating the landing of an early party of pioneers on November 13, 1851. Young and old enjoy the pleasures of this extraordinary, driftwood-strewn, city beach, whether in sunshine or storm. Favorite activities are beachcombing, picnicking, playing in the sand, strolling, and just sitting and looking. The Seattle World's Fair and Seattle Center rise across the bay beyond Duwamish Head. The television towers are on Queen Anne Hill.

(Right) Bridges of all sorts pay respect to the city's numerous waterways. Seen from the automobile bridge at Spokane Street, which serves all of West Seattle, this characteristic railroad counterweight bridge stands at attention over the Duwamish River. Attempts to enumerate the bridges of Seattle have failed, but it could well be known as the "City of Bridges." Seattle's most important industrial areas are served by the Duwamish, which has many large plants along its banks including Boeing Plants No. I and No. II, barely visible at the horizon.

To the north of Spokane Street is man-made industrial Harbor Island served by its two waterways. Ship repair and shipbuilding contribute a good share of the industrial activity as well as presenting an impressive reminder of our maritime heritage. Ships from many parts of the world visit Seattle, contributing their grace and beauty to the scene and bringing to the dreamer thoughts of romance and adventure in distant places.

The new Shilshole breakwater and boat harbor, just off the Puget Sound entrance to the Lake Washington Ship Canal, is a joy to sailors and landlubbers alike. Records show more than fifty thousand pleasure boats in the Seattle area, and the growing Shilshole moorage is recognition of the importance of boating as an amenity factor for the city. Public funds provided the breakwater and moorage. A stroll down its different floats to view the boats is a pleasure for visitors of all ages.

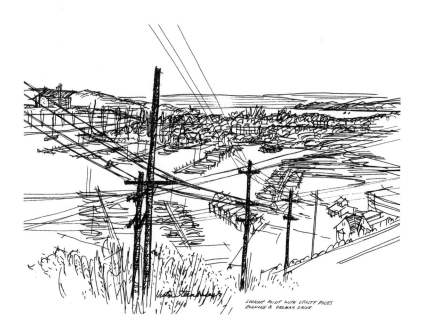

LOOKOUT POINT WITH UTILITY POLES
ROANOKE & DELMAR DRIVE

From a lookout point on North Capitol Hill, the yacht and house-boat haven of Portage Bay can be viewed. Beyond are the University of Washington, identified by its huge athletic stadium; Lake Washington; the hills; and the Cascade Range. It is a sweeping, thrilling panorama, with the contrasts between the picturesque moorages of the Seattle Yacht Club and the Queen City Yacht Club and the distant foliage, sky, and water textures. The utility poles in the foreground are a ubiquitous part of the Seattle scene, although the city is irretrievably committed to their ultimate elimination. A colony of fifty houseboats is being removed to make way for the Evergreen Bridge Expressway as it crosses over Portage Bay, but the houseboats along the west shore remain. There is much to be said about the houseboat way of life as a particularly characteristic element of Seattle life. Various forms of progress continue to threaten its damp existence, but as long as there is water in Seattle, some people will continue to enjoy living on it. For them, the houseboat provides a kind of home and community to their liking that cannot be found elsewhere. To the observer the colony is a romantic assortment of quaint dwellings forming patterns and texture along the water's edge—or is it the land's edge?

Victor Steinbrueck

The city of hills presents contrasts of light and dark values and changing textures in this view north toward the Arboretum and the University of Washington from Thirty-first Avenue East and East Pine Street in the Madrona district. Partly because it is not an unusual part of the city, it is recognizable as typical of the natural setting and characteristic urban pattern. Pleasantly steep rolling hills are surmounted by ordinary houses sometimes made a little special by adaptation to site and view. Portions of the hills considered too steep for development are still covered with greenery. The magnificent foliage of the Arboretum blends into the surrounding residential areas. Often a church or another high building on a promontory provides a landmark to orient the observer. Here it is the Catholic Holy Names Academy atop the eastern slope of Capitol Hill to the left. In the distance beyond the Arboretum are Meany Hotel, landmark of the University district, and the stadium of the University of Washington. Distant hills lose their textures as they fade into space.

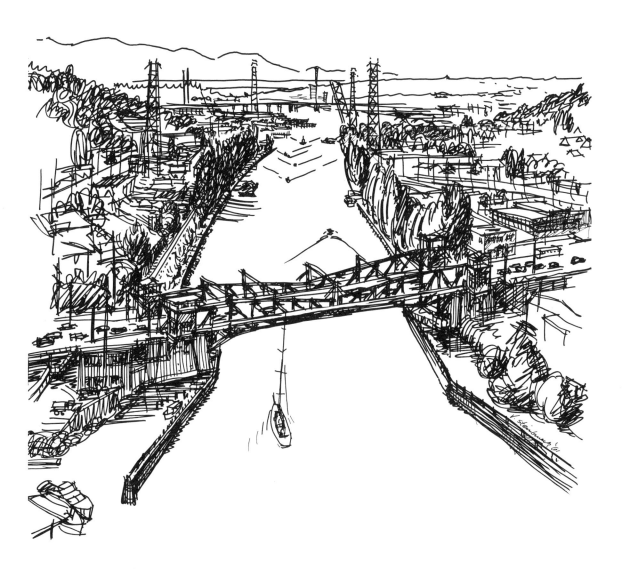

The Lake Washington Ship Canal was dug in 1917 to connect Lake Washington, Lake Union, and Puget Sound and aid in commercial development of the inland waters. While this purpose is still served, the most abundant activity has become that of pleasure boats passing to and from Puget Sound and its salt-water cruising world. Edges of Queen Anne, Magnolia, Ballard, and Fremont districts are defined by the waterway, which is fringed with commercial developments.

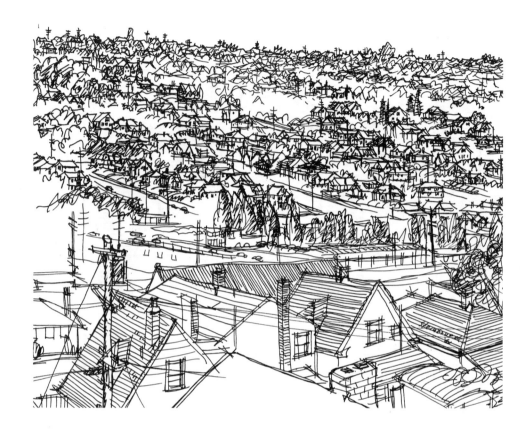

When one looks at the city as a whole, the series of patterns of building masses, trees, and yards are conceivable as textures. The hilly contours provide innumerable viewing places, and the "urban texture" of the surface is everywhere evident. The north slope of Queen Anne Hill rising from the Lake Washington Ship Canal presents this aspect of Seattle's physical environment in a most obvious and typical fashion. The texture is composed of gable- and hip-roofed middle-class houses, usually on grades a little above the street, with uniform yards and an abundant scattering of trees, and with the omnipresent thorns of utility poles crisscrossing to the skyline, which in this view is punctuated only by house, tree, and pole. Color plays an important role, adding to the richness of the scene.

Image of a City

This book is a series of sketches and thoughts about Seattle which together produce a larger, more comprehensive sketch. Pictures and sketches can only suggest, although perhaps by their very brevity, essentiality, and generality they may allow the observer to participate more fully in the experience of knowing and comprehending the city. Certainly no one ever fully knows the city because one's perception is always incomplete, subjective, and ever changing. The city itself is a theater in the large, presenting at every moment more than can be seen, more than can be heard, with changing views and settings waiting to be experienced. Nothing is experienced by itself or without the participation of the observer. The surroundings, the sequence of events, the associations with past experiences and history color and qualify the changing image. This book attempts to develop awareness of the esthetic, educational, and dramatic experience of the city, proposing the challenge that an urban environment should be worth what it costs the people.

Because of a particular combination of favorable conditions, Seattle is more than just a city; it is a very special, unique place. These favorable characteristics are its unsurpassed natural setting, combining greenery, hills, and water, and its proximity to the country and natural waterways; the pleasant, changing, temperate climate; and the adventurous, freedom-loving, friendly people who live here. The people have made and are making the city, and it in turn exercises its influences upon their destinies. Planners call the Puget Sound country an "amenities area"; in other words, it is a good place to live, work, and play. As time goes by, people must and will enhance its physical qualities through planning in order to increase their own happiness and cultural enjoyment, thereby incidentally causing economic appreciation as well. Building upon a most favorably endowed natural setting, devoted and enlightened citizens have made tremendous efforts, often with good results. Sometimes the situation caused favorable results merely because of abundant natural graces. Some results, as in all American cities, have been accidental, unplanned, and chaotic or ugly, but given the opportunity nature and man are correcting these mistakes. We like to believe that the favorable esthetic and cultural values are characteristic of Seattle, and the conflicts with these values will pass away.

When an individual is able to orient and relate himself to his environment, he is more likely to feel comfortable and enjoy his situation. This adjustment is partially dependent upon the person's perception and his emotional nature as well as upon the actual physical aspects of the spaces and forms in which he finds himself. Thus, Seattle's varied and readily identifiable natural and man-made features are both a pleasure and a source of emotional satisfaction since they provide abundant clues for comprehending the city and for orienting oneself. Among the significant aspects are panoramas, skylines, promontories, vistas, landmarks, open spaces, circulation paths or facilities, significant architectural masses, and urban textures. All of these features exert a tremendous influence upon one's experience of the city.

It is a basic premise of this book that esthetic experience is a part of everyday life, an essential human value, not a separate circumstance related only to the so-called fine arts. There is no one who is not affected by the quality of his environment. Living values that are a part of Seattle and the Puget Sound country exercise an irresistible power of attraction on most people who have been exposed to their charms.

One of the negative factors related to overdependence on nature for esthetic quality is the inclination to let nature take care of the situation or merely to accept what nature has to offer instead of meeting the challenge that it provides. Another unfortunate attitude is a lack of respect for the natural setting. Major changes in the contours of our city still show open wounds and scars and cannot be held to be unmitigated blessings and improvements. Elimination of Denny Hill to form the flat, formless Denny Regrade might be considered to demonstrate such callousness. Much of "suburbia" is guilty. The ruthless brutality of the latest freeways, expressways, and their structures in ignoring the qualities of the locations through which they move is an obvious example of short-sighted disregard for human and natural values in favor of narrow technical considerations of automobile movement.

A great city ought to have a well-defined cultural, social, and economic foundation that is expressed in the physical actuality of its form. Seattle contains many of the elements for this, although the appropriate expressive forms have not always been found. Parks and boulevards, museums, libraries, the public market, industrial areas, shopping districts, and other centers are meaningful expressions of the city's interests and activities. As these grow and mature, and our awareness of the human values in our environment increases, the city will move toward greatness.

The city should be considered as a work of art, with visual elements such as line, direction, proportion, shape, texture, value, color, mass, movement, and space related by repetition, gradation, contrast, variation, and rhythm to produce harmony, unity, interest, and discord. Since a work of art is both a thing in itself and a communication, content or meaning must also be included as an inherent and most vital part of the whole. The city is taken as a unified expression of social and functional values as well as esthetic ones. The clues for design are to be found within the activities and meaning of the city itself.

From the biased penpoint of this book, it seems clear that none has participated more effectively in forming the man-made physical urban environment than have architects. Other forces have found expression, of course, but the buildings and structures that provide the pattern and texture of the city are the result either of the work of architects or of their influence. It is true that much of the mass of building of any American city is accomplished without the full participation of the architect, but none is without his influence. When the culture is so well developed that fine architecture is the natural expression of the social climate, there will be more hope regarding man's destiny. In the past, greater vision and greater skill might have shaped a man-made environment worthy of its natural setting and human purpose. An interesting fantasy is to imagine what form Seattle might have had if some of its founders had been architects and philosophers. However, the formative years are still with this young city, and the vision of architects can help to create a broad, central design idea that will serve as an organizing force for our contemporary society. Civic design must be incorporated into a creative democratic public process of long-range urban planning, involving qualified, thoughtful experts from all areas of interest, but with public support brought about through widespread participation and understanding. This is now taking place in Seattle and its metropolitan region.

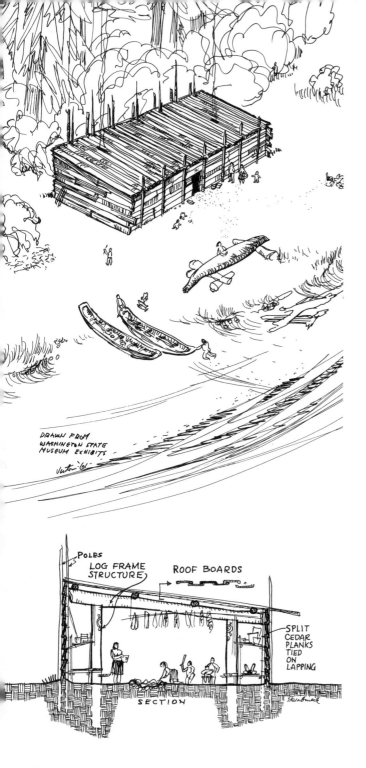

DRAWN FROM
WASHINGTON STATE
MUSEUM EXHIBITS

Victor '61

POLES
LOG FRAME
STRUCTURE
ROOF BOARDS

SPLIT
CEDAR
PLANKS
TIED
ON
LAPPING

SECTION

When the early white explorers and pioneers sailed up the northwest Pacific Coast and into Puget Sound, they were surprised to find large, well-made, wooden houses on the beaches near rivers and streams. Nowhere else were such houses built. Along the coast, the houses were often gable-roofed, but in Puget Sound the houses of the Salish were very low-pitched, shed-roofed structures. Of these none remain except in the memory of man. Usually the buildings were from twenty-five to forty feet wide and sixty to a hundred feet long, although Chief Seattle lived in a compartmented "long house" about nine hundred feet long on the beach at Suquamish. Solidly constructed of sturdy upright poles, beams, and rafters, the houses were sheathed with wide, long, split cedar planks. Roof boards were hollowed cedar planks in the shape of full-length tiles. The boards were tied on with cedar withes. Although they have not been recognized as such, these buildings are a prototype for contemporary curtain wall construction in which structure and exterior are independent of each other. A typical single dwelling was owned by one man, and the group who lived in the house were usually relatives. In winter the house was more than mere housing; it was a social center as well. Larger houses were occasionally used for potlatches—ceremonial festivals where gifts were bestowed on the guests and property was destroyed in a competitive show of wealth. In summer the permanent house was hardly used since everyone except the very old and the very young went to the favorite fishing camps.*

* Sketches and text derived from material at Washington State Museum.

The Puget Sound Salish summer camps must have been a source of enjoyment for those who left the permanent winter quarters in the plank houses. Most of the able-bodied people joined in rolling the mats and packing the canoes with their equipment. Canoe parties moved out in small groups to favored localities for fishing, shellfish gathering, berrying, root digging, and hunting, where the temporary mat shelters were erected. Simple A-frames or shed frames of poles were set up, and the sewn mats of cattail leaves were laid on the frames in overlapping shingle fashion. The houses were small and similar to present-day campers' tents, and the camps were mobile. People lived out of doors most of the time as we do while camping. The pleasant work of fishing, hunting, and gathering took place while the food was being dried or preserved in some manner for winter storage.*

Sketch and text derived from material at Washington State Museum.

DRAWN FROM SOURCES
AT WASHINGTON STATE MUSEUM

"Birthplace of Seattle"

"At this place on 13 November 1851 there landed from the Schooner Exact Captain Folger the little colony which developed into the City of Seattle. Children—Louise C. Denny, Lenora Denny, Rolland H. Denny, Alonzo Low, Mary Low, John Low, Minerva Low, Gertrude Boren, Laura Bell, Olive Bell, Virginia Bell, Lavinia Bell. Adults—Arthur A. Denny and wife, John N. Low and wife, Carson D. Boren and wife, William N. Bell and wife, Louisa Boren, David T. Denny, Charles C. Terry, Lee Terry. 'NEW YORK—ALKI' erected by Washington University State Historical Society 13 November 1905." So reads the inscription on the simple monument at Alki Avenue Southwest and Sixty-third Avenue Southwest.

Vctor Steinbrueck's
from records
of Seattle Historical Society

The landing party built a small cabin of logs which was to be one of the few of its kind in a growing mill town. Already in 1850, John C. Holgate, the first white settler, had selected a timber claim in the Duwamish Valley, now an industrial section. He was followed in September of 1851 by Luther Collins, Henry Van Asselt, and Jacob Maple, who also settled in the wilderness of Duwamish Valley near what has since become Georgetown. In 1852, the Alki pioneers moved across Elliott Bay and settled in the area that was to become Seattle's central business district. Early in 1852, Dr. David S. Maynard arrived and built a two-story house. Later in 1852, Henry L. Yesler moved in, and in March, 1853, at the present site of Pioneer Square, he started the sawmill that became the base of Seattle's economy. The names of these pioneers, who shaped Seattle's growth, appear on many streets, parks, and buildings, preserving Seattle's association with its past. Examples are the names of streets such as Bell Street, Denny Way, Boren Avenue, Terry Avenue, Holgate Street, Maple Street, Van Asselt Court, Maynard Avenue, Lenora Street, Virginia Street, Olive Way, Louisa Street, and Yesler Way. Most of the families had burial plots in the Lakeview cemetery on the north side of Capitol Hill, and their names can be seen there, too.

In the spring of 1853, Henry L. Yesler began operating his steam sawmill near the site of present-day Pioneer Square. As lumber was selling in California for sixty dollars a thousand board feet, the new community prospered. This was the first demonstration of how forest resources would be a primary resource in the growth of Seattle and the region. Production was thirty thousand board feet of lumber per day. The mill burned down a few times and was rebuilt. Both Indians and whites were employed; in fact, most of the Seattle pioneers worked for Yesler at one time or another. In 1888 the sawmill was moved out to the north shore of Union Bay where, after being burned out twice, it was abandoned. There have been many sawmills in Seattle. The largest at present is the Nettleton Timber Company Mill at West Waterway, capable of processing forty million board feet annually. Rafts of logs are towed in, sawed, and shipped by rail and cargo. The buildings are in simple heavy timber construction and are representative of the anonymous architecture of Seattle.

One of the best remaining examples of an authentic pioneer Seattle home is this small house at Fairview Avenue North and Mercer Street. Although it was not built until 1877, it is the simple, direct sort of house that was built here from the beginning and during the first thirty years of growth. Well built by ship's carpenter John T. Yarno, it has been lived in continuously by his daughter, Miss Margaret Yarno. She was seven years old when it was built, and the population was a few thousand. Board houses like this were built instead of log cabins because the sawmills almost preceded the people. This simple building is witness to the transition of a wilderness into a great city; unfortunately it is now doomed since it stands in the path of one of the new freeway approaches. Similar houses can be seen in the sketch of the Seattle waterfront in 1855 and are common in the views of 1870, 1878, and 1889 that follow. Others can still be found by exploration in older districts, especially south of Jackson Street in the vicinity of Chinatown.

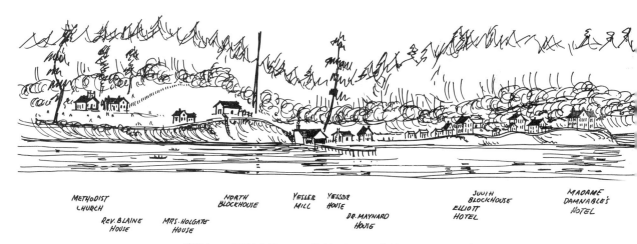

METHODIST
CHURCH

REV. BLAINE
HOUSE

MRS. HOLGATE
HOUSE

NORTH
BLOCKHOUSE

YESLER
MILL

YESLER
HOUSE

DR. MAYNARD
HOUSE

SOUTH
BLOCKHOUSE

ELLIOTT
HOTEL

MADAME
DAMNABLE'S
HOTEL

VIEW OF WATERFRONT, SEATTLE, WASHINGTON TERRITORY, 1855
SKETCHED IN 1961 FROM RECORDS OF SEATTLE HISTORICAL SOCIETY

The first church built in Seattle, at the southeast corner of Second Avenue and Columbia Street, appears in the waterfront view of 1855. Dedicated in May, 1855, it measured twenty-four by forty feet and was painted white, and it was commonly known as "The White Church." The Reverend David Blaine was the minister, and his wife, Catherine Blaine, taught school in the church. It was the only church in the community for ten years. In 1870 the congregation was inspired, probably by other churches, to add a steeple and more sophisticated architectural details. Other churches of ancient vintage and similar size and character still stand in Port Townsend and Port Gamble.

In 1853 Dr. Maynard sold four lots at the northeast corner of Third Avenue and Washington Street to the Roman Catholic Church, but it was not until 1867 that Father Francis Xavier Prefontaine came to Seattle and established a parish that resulted in building a church, Our Lady of Good Help, dedicated in 1870.

When the opportunity was presented, enterprising citizens got together and pledged ten acres of land required for "locating and establishing" a Territorial University in Seattle. The site was a knoll where the Olympic Hotel now stands, at Fifth Avenue and University Street. Records show that John Pike, a carpenter, was paid for the architecture and for framing and closing in the building. It was two-storied, porticoed in the Greek Revival manner. In November of 1861, instruction was begun with thirty-seven pupils—one college and thirty-six lower grade students. Economic considerations and the need for more space forced the university to move to its present location in 1895. The four columns that graced the portals of the old building were brought along in 1908 and located in the Sylvan Theater, where they remain as the traditional symbol of the University of Washington. Since its founding, the university has played an increasingly important role in the intellectual, cultural, and even economic growth of Seattle and the area.

Seattle's first public school was a plain, unadorned, wooden two-story building facing Third Avenue between Madison and Spring streets. It was opened on August 15, 1870. Previously homes and churches had been used. Catherine Blaine was the first teacher at the new Central School.

In 1870, Harper's New Monthly *published an illustrated article, "The Mediterranean of the Pacific," describing a boat trip in Puget Sound waters. Seattle was not at that time the most impressive of towns although the entire area was highly lauded for its climate and beauty. Encounters with the Indians were described in detail. An engraving depicting the Seattle waterfront shows many of the same buildings that appear in the 1855 view. The homes are simple wood siding pioneer homes similar to the Yarno house, and there is a generous amount of open space. The Territorial University building seems to have been erased at the upper left of the engraving.*

SEATTLE, WASHINGTON TERRITORY, 1870

41

Looking south from Second Avenue and Pine Street in 1878, the town is seen to be changing to a more sophisticated place but is still a village. The population is approximately two thousand. Unadorned pioneer houses are prevalent, but decorated porches with a few pretty details are beginning to appear. The two-story house in the foreground is almost identical to the still existing Yarno house.

The only remaining example of an early pioneer hotel is the old Kalmar Hotel at Sixth Avenue and James Street. Built in 1881, it appears in the Seattle view of 1889 as the Western Hotel. With its pumpkin-colored wooden siding and band-sawn details, it has been a picturesque part of Seattle's personality. Much of the Seattle's history has been viewed from its wide veranda, but now it is being destroyed to make room for the freeway.

Built in 1879 at Fifth Avenue and Madison Street, the David C. Kellogg house was moved to 1327 Boren Avenue in 1903 when the site was given over to the Seattle Public Library. The interesting form and brown stained siding are in pleasant contrast with its more imposing and recent neighbors. The unpretentious quality of its architecture is commendable as an example of early day mansions, while the Lohse house (facing page) presents a more exuberant attitude. At 619 James Street, just uphill from the Kalmar Hotel, it is a fine specimen of imaginative use of the ornament of the day in a middle-class home. Architecture was becoming visually more decorative as the town became more worldly.

619

Victor Steinbruick
1960

hs A House - C. 1883
9 James Street

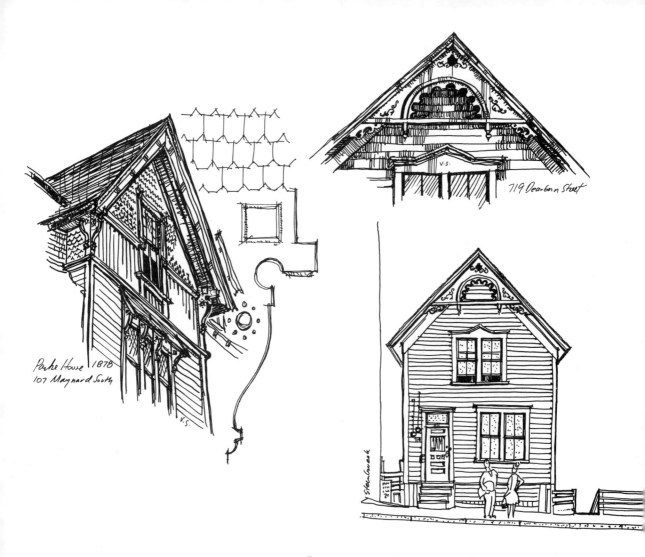

Parke House 1878
107 Maynard South

719 Dearborn Street

Imaginative and creative use by carpenters of wood details and patterns in the decade before 1889 are demonstrated in this gable detail of the Parke house at Seventh Avenue and Yesler Way, and on the façade and gable of the small house at 719 South Dearborn Street. This charming little house is almost identical with the Yarno house except for the sympathetic addition of decorative details. In the 1889 view there were many such homes, some of which are waiting to be rediscovered.

Contrasting with the old in a location associated with the past is the striking new Bayview Manor retirement home with its impressively clean, sweeping structure. Private balconies are continuous and afford the occupants a dramatic panorama of Elliott Bay. John Graham and Company, Architects and Engineers, produced this specialized contemporary building. It replaced the historic old Kinnear home, which had stood in its original glory in the parklike setting since 1887.

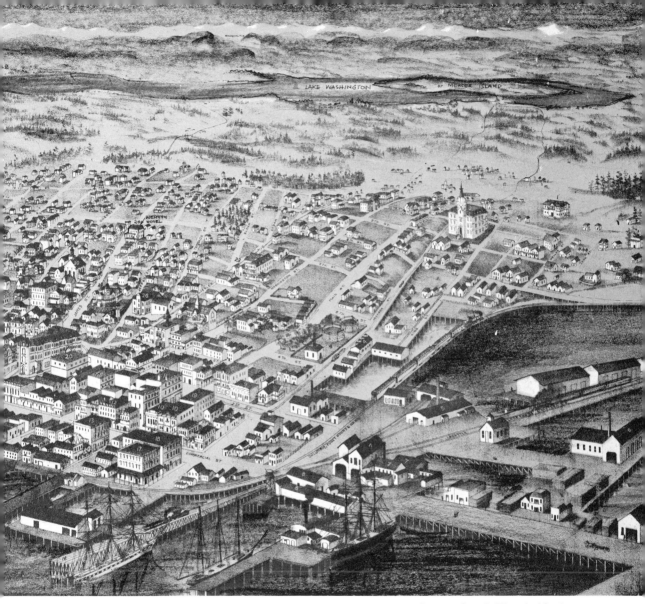

Courtesy Seattle Historical Society

SEATTLE VIEW, 1889

This view looking east up Yesler Way from Pioneer
Square on June 7, 1889, shows the smoldering
ruins that were part of the business district completely destroyed by the devastating fire of the
previous day. The city went to work with great
determination to rebuild immediately, concentrat-
ing in the general area of First Avenue and Yesler
Way.

FIRE DEPARTMENT HEADQUARTERS·

1890

Architects Saunders and Houghton produced this strategically located fire department headquarters immediately after the Seattle Fire to insure adequate protection for the rebuilding city. Its associations with the past influence our interest and concern for this building, another of those in the path of the freeway, at Seventh Avenue and Columbia Street. It must have provided a thrilling sight as the fire horses and engines moved out through its doors to the scene of a fire. The architecture is derivative from traditional style while still maintaining an originality in detail.

Looking down through the gray actinic glass of the elegant new Norton Building's Harbor Club, one sees Pioneer Square and the old buildings of the present Skid Road on First Avenue South. Most of the buildings were built immediately following the Fire and consequently have a consistency in character and scale not commonly found. Pioneer Square has a special place in the heart of Seattle, and there is hope of bringing it back into the life of the city although it receives little respect from its occupants. Proposals for restoration have been made by private interests, although government assistance may be required. If the project is to be successful, the planning must include a Skid Road Park nearby for displaced Skid Road characters. This otherwise rundown area demonstrates the principle that a cohesive group of buildings presents a quality beyond that of a single building.

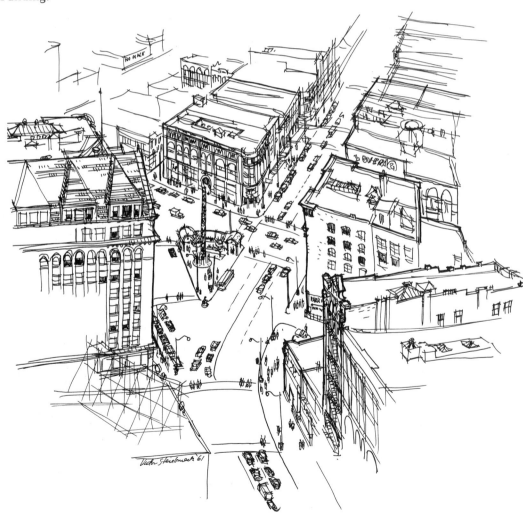

Austin A. Bell Building
2324 First Avenue
(Belltown)
V. Stangroote

Detail
Mutual Life Building
94 Yesler Way

Northern Hotel · 1889
115 First Avenue South
TERRY DENNY

Rich and flavorsome old buildings associated with the pioneers stand proudly even though they are neglected at present. A fresh look at the interesting details and fine masonry is rewarding and suggests possibilities for sympathetic restoration.

PIONEER BUILDING
LOAN
V.S.
Henry Yesler's building · 1890
First Avenue + Yesler Way

MAYNARD BUILDING

David S.
Maynard Building · 1892
First Avenue South and Washington Street

53

After the Fire, Angus Mackintosh rebuilt his "Safe Deposit Building" housing the Merchants National Bank below six stories of hotel rooms named the Kenneth Hotel. At that time the bank was the state's fourth largest financial institution, with deposits of more than $700,000. It was said of its facilities that "the quarters were elegantly furnished and excelled by none on the coast." After the turn of the century, the bank closed its doors and Seattle's first true motion-picture theater, the Dream, was located in its place. The hotel now serves mainly an American Indian population, while the pioneer vaults finally closed after a spectacular robbery in the early 1950's. There is little to show of its past elegance, yet the narrow building still presents a delightful termination to Cherry Street with its ornateness further adorned by the tracery of a 1906 iron fire escape. This symbol of the colorful past of the city cries out for sympathetic restoration.

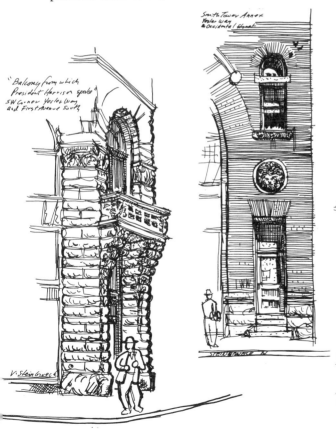

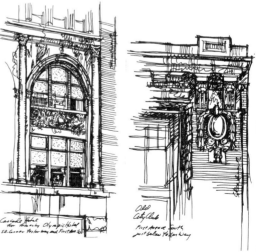

Post Street below First Avenue at Columbia Street presents an interesting possibility for development in connection with a rejuvenated Pioneer Square. Consistent and harmonious brickwork in walls and paving combines with the narrow street to form an ideal pedestrian lane. The buildings that front on First Avenue show heavy iron hinges and often fire shutters at the windows as a result of precautions following the Fire.

The totem pole and iron pergola in Pioneer Square are picturesque elements that should be preserved in any improvement, which must also include sympathetic redecorating of such buildings as the early vintage Olympia Hotel, now known as the Cascade Hotel or "flophouse."

Victor Steinbrueck '6

The Skid Road, doubtful haven of society's derelicts and
misfits, is interesting architecturally and otherwise, but de-
pressing to the humanitarian. Here mankind seems to have
lost respect for itself. The earthquake of 1949 damaged
many of the buildings, and others have been torn
down to make way for more lucrative parking lots. This
view, looking north on Occidental Avenue near Washington Street, in the summer of 1961, shows the old Seattle
Hotel being wrecked. The Norton Building and Hoge Building loom beyond. Yesler Way was originally called Mill
Street, and logs were skidded down the road, at first by hand
and later with teams of oxen. This was the original Skid
Road, and its location was the tough "below the line" section of a pioneering mill town.

Views up or down sloping streets are much more satisfying than looking into endless avenues leveling into the distant horizon. This is one of the visual pleasures of moving about Seattle. Yesler Way, the old Mill Street down to Yesler's mill at the location of this sketch, has been a picturesque thoroughfare since the beginning. For many years, cable cars clanged along from Pioneer Square to Leschi Park. Downtown streets change their direction at Yesler Way to be square with the world again. Smith Tower presides at Second Avenue. Up the hill is Yesler Terrace Public Housing Project at Broadway on a site formerly known as "Profanity Hill" because of the language used by the teamsters as they drove their teams up the steep grade. The now demolished Seattle Hotel and its predecessor, the Occidental Hotel, were always the quality hotels of early Seattle. Contrasts are interesting, and Yesler Way has many.

59

Victor Steinbrueck — August, 1961

If Seattle were to lose all of its flavorsome old buildings, one could still visit Port Townsend on the Strait of Juan de Fuca for the ultimate in Victorian architecture. Port Townsend is a veritable architectural museum, with many buildings and homes of the 1880's still in excellent condition. As the port of entry, it was the booming "key city" of the Northwest until economic failures thwarted its destiny in 1890. Now the town is moving forward to a new and interesting future as a recreational and cultural center, with its fine old buildings providing a unique setting. The street scene shows the main business street with its clean, wind-swept façades.

Perhaps the most elegant and surely the most appealing of the old mansions in the Puget Sound country is the Bartlett house, built in 1883 and now graciously lived in by Dr. and Mrs. Harry Johnson. Preservation of Victorian Port Townsend is precious to Seattle and the entire Puget Sound country.

Not the only old building of character that has been sacrificed to the freeway, this 1890 vintage Victorian apartment at 908 Eastlake was a fine example of creative and imaginative designing within a style. The façade shows a surprisingly adept use of large plate glass areas combined with light, graceful balconies. The unusual colored glass and the varied, original ornament and pattern were a pleasure to behold. Architects particularly enjoyed its proportions and relations of voids and solids, which seemed to prophesy present contemporary design.

Old Queen Anne Town has become Queen Anne Hill, and only a few Queen Anne houses remain although once there were many. At Warren Avenue and North Aloha Street was this quaint old mansion of the 1890's, built by the Stimsons. It was demolished in 1962 to make way for an apartment house, and thus another reminder of Seattle's past was lost. The imaginative form and exuberant detail expressed the elegance and confidence of a vital period in Seattle's growth.

725 - 21st Avenue

1515 & 1517 Yesler Way

124 - 23rd Avenue South

304 - 28th Ave. S.

2414 Jackson Street

Crowded between brick buildings at 1427 Boren Avenue is this fanciful example of residential Victorian carpenter Gothic, one of the most interesting and apparently sound of the rare few remaining. It could be made delightfully attractive by sympathetic preservation as it stands today.

East Madison in the area of Twenty-second Avenue East is a motley district of varied and nondescript buildings except for this impressive old mansion of 1900 with its neighboring chestnut trees. Its broad veranda and large, decorative, shingled gable dominate the neighborhood. The turned-out edge of the gable shingles where they meet the rake of the roof is most interesting along with the delicately carved "Gothic" details. It is known that this was the early home of a wealthy and prominent madam, Lou Graham. Because of its architectural value, it is worthy of restoration and preservation.

Shingle-style houses are very appropriate to this climate and region, as suggested by these fine, old—but not well-kept—houses at 727 Boren Avenue and at 1107 and 1111 Columbia Street. The techniques of shingle work on roofs and sidewalls, demonstrating a good use of wood, made possible more original forms than could be developed with other types of wood or masonry exteriors. The two-story arched gable window and balcony detail are good architectural fun. These houses seem quite contemporary in spite of their sixty years.

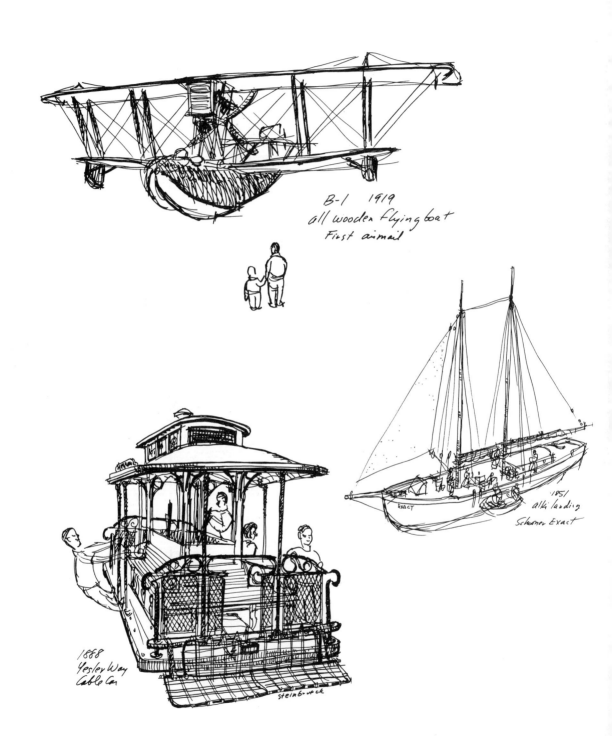

B-1 1919
all wooden flying boat
First airmail

1851
alki landing
Schooner Exact

EXACT

1888
Yesler Way
Cable Car

steinbruck

MUSEUM OF HISTORY + INDUSTRY
Steinbrueck '60

The free public Museum of History and Industry with its parent
body, the Seattle Historical Society, is the active repository for many
historical documents and artifacts of this locality. As an effective
center of historical information, it holds a high position of respect
and interest in the community. The original main building shown
was designed by architect Paul Thiry in 1950, with wings added later
by other architects. Executed in a direct, simple, and refined manner, it is excellent contemporary architecture in a pleasant setting
adjacent to the University of Washington Arboretum. The Evergreen Bridge Expressway will pass through the present approach
shown, and the entrance is to be relocated.

The Seattle Art Museum was presented to the city by Dr. Richard Fuller and his mother in 1932. Carl F. Gould, Sr., was the architect of this important civic building with its dignified, clean façade and luxurious interior enclosed court, which were architecturally far in advance of their time. In its Volunteer Park setting it overlooks Elliott Bay to the Olympic Mountains. Under the continuing leadership of Dr. Richard Fuller, the museum has dominated the art activities of the city for three decades. The Asian art collection is most outstanding. Chinese marble sculptures at the approach are a source of visual and tactile pleasure for young citizens.

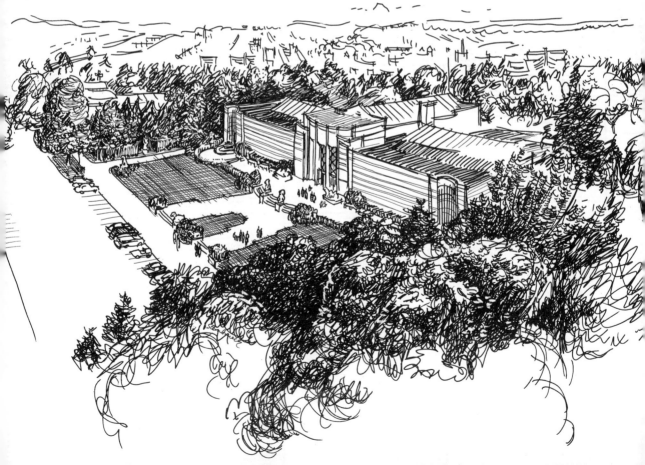

Civic pride has been bolstered by the fresh and dignified new Seattle Public Library at Fourth Avenue and Spring Street, which was completed in 1959. It was designed by architects Bindon and Wright, with Decker, Christenson, and Kitchin as associates. Seattle's real civic interest in the quality and growth of its libraries has been given expression by the incorporation into this building of the work of outstanding local artists. George Tsutakawa's fine bronze fountain enhances the street corner as well as the building. James FitzGerald's glass and bronze screen, Glen Alps's copper screen, and Ray Jensen's sculptured figures are worthy of any city's pride.

71

First Hill is an apartment district that also includes a number of large hospitals and related facilities. It began as the finest residential area of Seattle, and at the turn of the century its large and elegant mansions carried the names of many of the city's first families. Changing times and city growth wiped out most of these homes to make room for multistory luxury apartments of the various decades. The older apartments have small windows and large rooms, while the more recent have larger windows and smaller rooms. All enjoy the view, which continues to change as one building becomes the view for another. The Sunset Club, built in 1915, was designed by architect Joseph Cote. Its dignified presence contrasts nicely with the larger, more recent structures. This is also true of the older University Club, formerly the residence of M. V. B. Stacy.

During the past few years Capitol Hill has experienced tremendous growth in less-than-luxury types of apartments similar to this concrete structure. At first glance, the apartments appear to be consistent with the clean, direct approach associated with contemporary architecture, but a closer look or visit shatters the illusion. The open outside corridors, sewing together all of the individual units, comply with building codes but not with human needs for privacy and enjoyment. The corridors pass in front of large "view" windows in the living rooms of the individual apartments so that occupants and passersby are equally in view. Most tenants close their blinds and look for another apartment when their lease runs out. Inadequate parking is another problem of this plethora of new "pigeonhole" apartments, which were hurriedly built before 1959 to avoid a zoning law change.

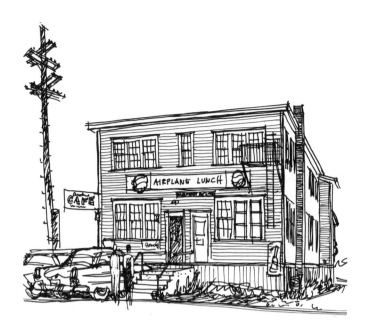

Anyone living near Seattle finds it easy to believe that Boeing Airplane Company is the largest manufacturer of aircraft on this planet. Since its founding in 1917, Boeing's growth has been synonymous with that of aircraft. The fact that more Seattleites are dependent on aircraft for their livelihood than on any other industry indicates that the future of the city is closely allied with that of Boeing. A visit to Boeing's Plant I at the original site on the Duwamish Waterway presents an interesting contrast with the vast industrial empire at Plant II as seen from the Boeing Field flight tower. This old "Airplane Lunch" building outside the Plant I entrance now seems rather insignificant although it was one of the first additional structures built by Boeing while it was only partially utilizing an existing shipyard plant during World War I.

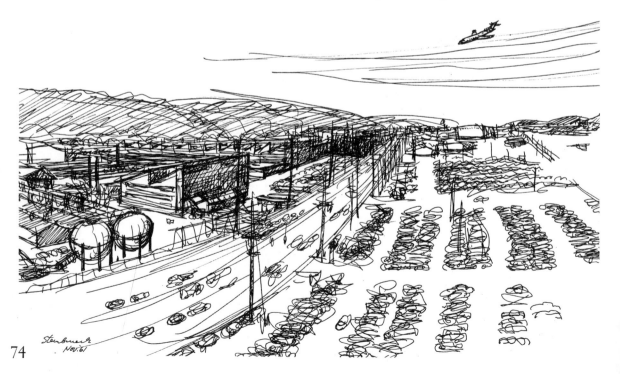

74

As the center of the region's intellectual and cultural activities, the University of Washington has greatly influenced the city's existence. Need for expansion and skyrocketing downtown property values pushed the university out to a wooded site on the shores of Union Bay in 1893 with the building of Denny Hall by architects Saunders and Lawton. Recently modernized inside and restored outside, the building is still used for classrooms and faculty offices and still gives pleasure both by its visual quality and by its assocation with tradition.

Something of the natural character of the original setting remains in this short path through the H. C. Henry memorial grove of dogwood trees just north of Anderson Hall, home of the College of Forestry. There is still an abundance of trees and shrubs, and the campus seems to be a calm, green city within the city.

Lewis Hall, on the campus of the university, was built in 1896 at a cost of twenty-five thousand dollars by architects Josenhans and Allen. Originally a dormitory, it has been remodeled several times for other purposes. Architecturally, it has qualities of honesty, simplicity, pleasing proportions, and scale that in an unpretentious way surpass the attributes of more aggressive recent buildings. The lofty Washington elm is a scion of the original elm under which General Washington first took command of the American army in 1775 at Cambridge, Massachusetts.

Old Parrington Hall looks down Rainier Vista past the library, the administration building, and Frosh Pond to majestic Mount Rainier, ninety miles away. The "collegiate Gothic" style, as advocated and developed by architect Carl Gould, was adhered to from 1914 until 1957, presenting exterior aspects of group harmony and unity that are being reinforced by the more diversified character of newer buildings in which freedom to experiment architecturally has been allowed. At present, under the guidance of an architectural advisory committee composed of such architects as William W. Wurster, Minoru Yamasaki, and Dean Arthur P. Herrman, architecture and campus planning appropriate to this great university's academic goals are being sought.

The ecclesiastically scaled vertical Gothic library was created in 1928 by architect Carl F. Gould to form an idealistic and visual focus for the university. The grand scheme for the huge building complex included a high stack tower, rising as the crowning spire of the campus, which was not expected to be built at once, nor was it. The imposing façade, expressing the cathedral-like main reading room, has been symbolic of the university. Plans for a colossal addition to the north and east are now being executed. The architecture will be somewhat different in character but is intended to harmonize with the old style.

Because of its daring engineering, imposing size, and unusually dramatic forms, the university's stadium has become a landmark since its construction in 1946. Stoddard and Huggard were the architects, and Sigmund Ivarsson was the structural engineer. The structure is impressive, especially when a winning football team fills it to its capacity of fifty-five thousand.

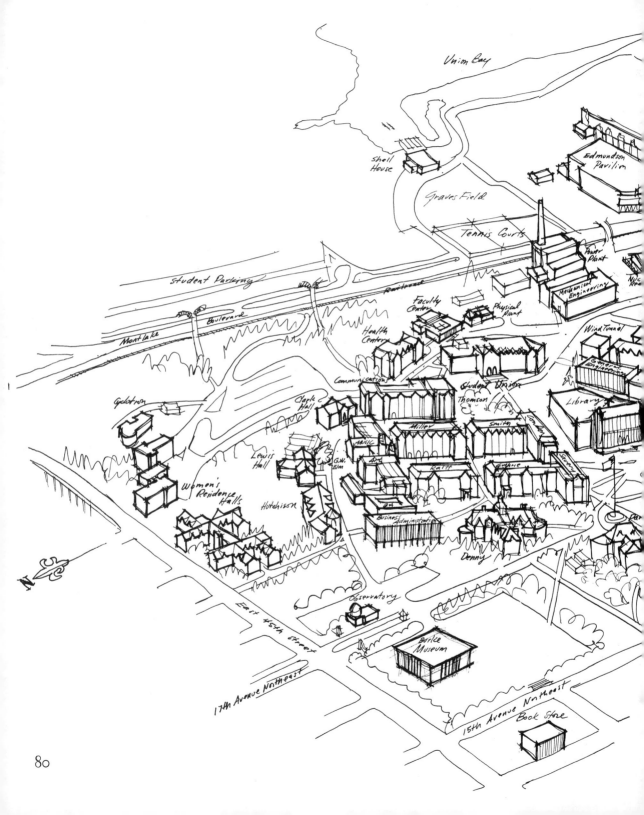

Union Bay

Shell House

Edmundson Pavilion

Graves Field

Tennis Courts

Power Plant

Student Parking

Railroad

Mechanical Engineering

Mic Kee

Boulevard

Faculty Center

Physical Plant

Wind Tunnel

Montlake

Health Center

Communication

Student Union

Thomson

Library

Civil Engineering

Cyclotron

Clark Hall

Miller

Smith

Gowen

Lewis Hall

MSE

Art

Raitt

Savery

Women's Residence Halls

G.W. Elm

Guthrie

Hutchison

Business Administration

Denny

N

Observatory

East 45th Street

Burke Museum

17th Avenue Northeast

15th Avenue Northeast

Book Store

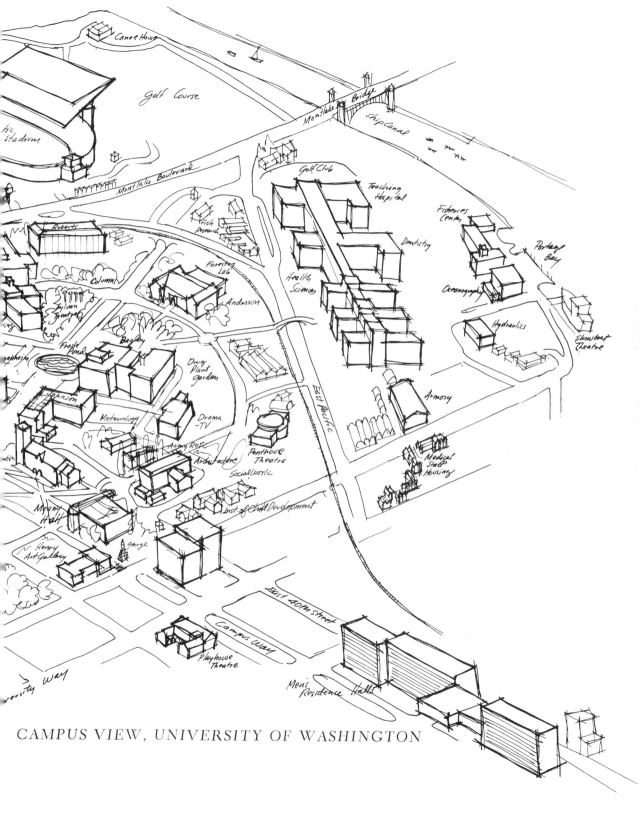

CAMPUS VIEW, UNIVERSITY OF WASHINGTON

The Tenth Avenue Mall of Seattle University is a comfortable pedestrian space alongside the Liberal Arts Building. Architect John Maloney produced this concrete building in 1941 and has been the architect of all campus work since that time. Seattle University was founded in 1891 by the Fathers of the Society of Jesus, but the institution has not always been at the present location. There are approximately four thousand students, with five thousand forecast by 1965. The "Old Science" Building was built largely by contributed labor in 1893 and is a unique element in the architecture of the compact campus which has grown up within the grid pattern of the city streets. The severity of these site restrictions has forced a closeness and regularity of spaces between buildings that is friendly and pleasant as contrasted with the vast and often uncomfortably irregular spaces of other campuses.

Smith Tower is an example of a high, vertical building that has become a symbol and a landmark for a city. Built in 1914 to anchor the commercial district to the south end of the central business district, it serves that purpose and also stands as a monumental object in the skyline. The unique and rather ungainly form immediately orients the citizen as it comes into view. If its superficial ornament and ostentatious amassment are disregarded, it compares well with its younger brothers in lightness and airiness and in structural expression. It is well placed to relate visually to the gap that separates "Profanity Hill" from Beacon Hill when they are seen from a distance.

At dusk, the campanile of St. Mark's Cathedral in Venice, which was borrowed by the Northern Pacific for its depot at Fourth Avenue and Jackson Street, makes a repetitious composition with the higher Smith Tower. Each is given more interest by the support of the other.

Another unusual view of the Smith Tower is the amusing one presented when one approaches down Yesler Way near Sixteenth Avenue. Only the tower top is visible above Yesler Terrace, and a strange sense of elevation is experienced.

The Northern Life Tower, built in 1929, is a well-designed high building commanding respect as an impressive element in the downtown skyline as well as for its excellent architecture. Its size and form make it immediately recognizable and help to orient the observer in its locality. Vertically emphasized piers and setback forms are suggestive of our rugged nearby mountains. With its fine ornament and brickwork that is graded in color and value as it goes into the sky, the building masses into an inspiring form that is a credit to the talent of its designer Joseph W. Wilson, who was an associate of the architectural firm of A. H. Albertson.

Victor Steinbrueck Nov 59

The elegant new Norton Building of 1960 is a sharp and definite addition to the city's skyline with its orderly aluminum and black glass skin. It compares well with recent high buildings built anywhere and seems to approach the ultimate in curtain wall design. From street level, reflections of nearby older buildings lend enjoyable contrasts. The luxurious off-street entrance court with its art work lends a welcome quality to the vicinity, suggesting the need for open spaces in the central area. Bindon and Wright were the architects with Skidmore, Owings, and Merrill as associates.

The stately, new, white marble Washington Building has added its rectangular form to the skyline, contrasting in form and color with the other high buildings. During its construction the city was afforded the interesting experience of observing the process of change as the old, classic-style post office was destroyed and this monumental structure was erected. The glass-caged lobby is made much more luxurious and individual through the addition of the large, abstract bronze sculpture by local artist James FitzGerald. Art work of quality is becoming an essential element in Seattle's new buildings. This was built in 1960, with Naramore, Bain, Brady, and Johanson as the architects.

87

Marine Hospital
August '61

Two similar architectural landmarks of kindred style and form
guard the man-made gap between
"Profanity Hill" and Beacon Hill.
These buildings are visible from
many locations because of promontory positions which give added
emphasis to their readily identifiable forms. The original buff-
colored brick building of the
King County Harborview Hospital
was built in 1929 by architects
Thomas, Grainger, and Thomas.
Architects Bebb and Gould associated with John Graham, Sr., in
the design of the orange-brown
brick Marine Hospital, built in
1934 on Beacon Hill.

ST. MARKS EPISCOPAL CATHEDRAL

Two churches that occupy appropriately high places in Seattle's skyline are St. Mark's Episcopal Cathedral and St. James Catholic Cathedral. Both have become familiar landmarks. The imposing pile of massive concrete forms of St. Mark's atop Capitol Hill was built in 1930 from plans by San Francisco architect Arthur Brown. The building was fortunately never completed so that its massiveness is further emphasized by the exposed concrete. The twin towers of St. James Cathedral hover symbolically over the central business district. Skillfully arranged in the eclectic tradition, the architecture is refined and dignified, although derivative, as was the custom during the first half of this century.

An architectural and community landmark because of its size and form, the Edmond Meany Hotel in the University district was built in 1931 from the plans of architect R. C. Reamer. Representative of the most progressive design of that era, the exposed reinforced concrete tower, with all the rooms enjoying corner windows, became the prototype for many other towers. Integral ornamentation is interesting for its conscious restraint and relation to form. The work of several local artists was incorporated into the interiors.

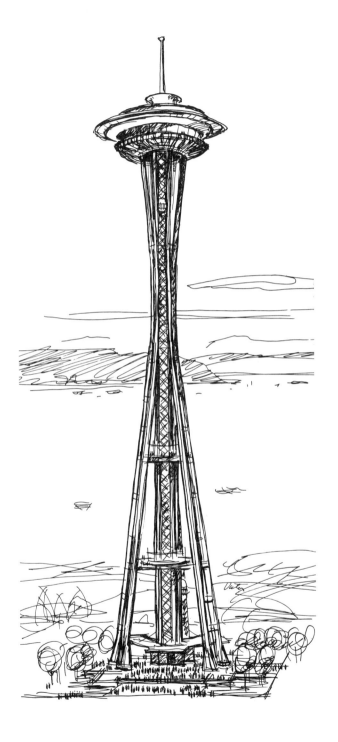

Seattle has gained another land-mark and symbol as a result of the Seattle World's Fair of 1962 with the erection of the six-hundred-foot restaurant and observation tower called the Space Needle. Rising two hundred feet above the highest hill, it would be recognized as a landmark because of its height alone since it is visible from many locations. Although a higher position, perhaps atop Queen Anne Hill or Duwamish Head, would have been more spectacular, the present site is surprisingly pleasant in the city-scape as an accent to the gap between Elliott Bay and Lake Union. The graceful form, which repeats the hour-glass shape of the city, is derived more from esthetic sources than from structural inspiration. The firm of John Graham and Company, Architects and Engineers, developed the project for the privately owned Space Needle Corporation as an extremely feasible financial enterprise.

One of the many locations that could be
developed as lookout points is the city-
owned Magnolia water reservoir at Twenty-
seventh Avenue West and West Bertona
Street. The panoramic view to the northeast across Salmon Bay and Fisherman's
Wharf includes the residential communities of Ballard and Phinney Ridge, with
lumber mills and boating activities enliven-
ing the scene.

Through a fortunate geographic circumstance, Rainier Valley sights directly at white-capped Mount Rainier, which the Indians called "The Mountain That Is God." The early city layout allowed Rainier Avenue to develop its vista toward that distant majesty. Later-day utilitarians have erected another series of vertical elements that have come to symbolize the city to many. Thus the magnificent symbol of nature is viewed through man's need for economical distribution of a basic commodity. For a full appreciation of the repetitious composition of crossed verticals connected by their catenary webs, the "Black Forest" of Beacon Hill should be visited.

At the juncture of Beacon Avenue South and South
Columbian Way stands the "Black Forest," containing many board feet of vertical lumber scratch-
ing the heavens. The view is completely dominated by the slender black objects and their inter-
twined webs. Of course it will not always be thus.

94

The central business district is approached from the south through industrial areas that have definite architectural qualities because of the direct, straightforward industrial construction, built to serve a working purpose. An aspect of harmony is achieved that is less apparent elsewhere. There is, however, an impersonal, severe quality, common to similar areas in other cities, which appears to be caused by the lack of pedestrian spaces, the dominance of automotive considerations, and the unkempt, unimproved, raw, empty land. There are outstanding exceptions, such as Sick's Breweries, at 3100 Airport Way South, with its well-kept, landscaped surroundings.

Another district lacking a sense of place because of the dominance of objects rather than of people and human spaces is the Denny Regrade, now a used car and motel center. The project of lowering and leveling Denny Hill was begun in 1906, and a remaining portion was leveled in 1929 and 1930. Thus a noble knoll was sluiced into Elliott Bay for a considerable sum of money, supposedly to expedite growth of the central business district.

One of the earliest American approaches to the consolidation of new shopping areas in convenient locations, with an appropriate scheme for the separation of people and automobiles, was developed in 1950 by John Graham and Company, Architects and Engineers, at Northgate Shopping Center. The interior pedestrian malls are a pleasant relief from conflict with automobile traffic and have been nicely landscaped. Plans are under way for further development of the malls with arcades and other improvements. There is an obvious suggestion here for the betterment of existing neighborhood shopping districts.

One of the most justifiably popular neighborhood shopping centers is that of the University district. Proximity to the University of Washington, which forms its economic base, has also given it a special character and color. In 1955, studies and proposals were made for the development of University Way as a shopper's mall, for solutions to parking problems, and for other amenities. Such developments would allow existing neighborhood shopping centers to compete with the newer centers. Often the older shops have a more personal and special nature than is possible in completely new developments. Parking problems must be solved, however, and the complete separation of automobile and pedestrian must be accomplished for the improvement of established shopping districts.

Typical neighborhood shopping districts are illustrated by the West Seattle Junction (above) and old Georgetown (below). West Seattle is thriving as an active group of small and varied specialty shops catering to the middle-class area that it serves. Georgetown experienced its heyday before and during World War I, when breweries and shipyards were booming. Georgetown's shopping center is interesting architecturally because of the two-block-long enclosed space of Twelfth Avenue South, dominated by the old brewery malt house beyond. Early Georgetown and South Park are changing from working-class residential neighborhoods to small manufacturing and industrial areas, with gigantic Boeing dominating the scene. Many present neighborhoods began early as separate towns and later merged their identities with that of Seattle. Some of these are Belltown, Interbay, Fremont, Edgewater (Wallingford), Latona, Ravenna, Yesler (Union Bay), Georgetown, Ballard, West Seattle, and Brooklyn (University).

Chinatown, with a little of the color of the
East and much of the clutter of the West,
has a fair sampling of Asian and colored mi-
norities not yet fully absorbed into the life
of the city. Chinese and Japanese restaurants
are numerous, and many are of excellent
quality, offering some of the best menus to
be found in Seattle. The campanile of the
Northern Pacific Railroad Depot serves as a
landmark for the location, while shops, markets, and people contribute the foreign accent.

99

The intersection of Third Avenue and Pike Street presents a busy cross section of people and architecture. The two big ten-cent stores generate business for each other and for adjoining shops. City transit is most active here, with many transfer points nearby. The uphill vista of Pike Street is pleasant in form but uninteresting in detail. Trolley wires provide a visual canopy to the scene of commonplace architecture and busy throngs. To know the face of Seattle's people, stand at this corner and observe.

The new Washington Building, the White-Henry-Stuart Building, and the 1411 Fourth Avenue Building at Fourth and Union combine to present a representative picture of Seattle's business district. The 1411 Fourth Avenue Building is one of the distinguished edifices produced in the office of architect R. C. Reamer during the booming twenties. Sharp and original detailing is apparent. This locality establishes the quality of the city's business environment. The lamppost with its automobile symbols suggests that such "street furniture" may play an important role in the observer's impression of the city.

101

American cities generally contain motley assortments of unrelated, inharmonious objects serving public and utilitarian purposes on the streets. The discordant variety of these elements may symbolize civil departmental relationships as well as lack of esthetic considerations. Although the Municipal Art Commission is now concerned with the appearance of our street furniture, little progress has been achieved. This is unfortunate since people are more aware of these objects than of the larger aspects of the cityscape.

The alley between Fourth and Fifth avenues, south of Westlake, has been suggested as an ideal location for the development of a pedestrian shopping lane. From Westlake past Pine Street to Union Street, and through the archways of the White-Henry-Stuart Building to the University Street entrance of the Olympic Hotel, is the path for a pleasantly arcaded shopping lane.

Rhodes of Seattle, with its arcade off the street, has already demonstrated that such a space has an attraction for the shopper on foot. Even hurrying pedestrians, bound elsewhere, come in from the street to walk the length of its comfortable, satisfying enclosure.

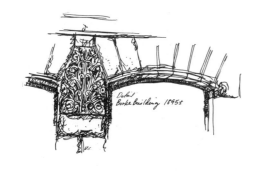

Detail
Burke Building 1895±

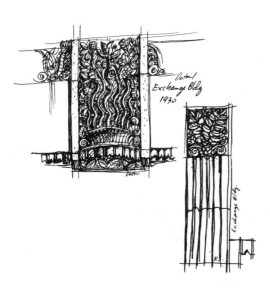

Detail
Exchange Bldg
1930

Exchange Bldg.

The changing character of Seattle's architecture stands exposed at Second Avenue from Marion Street to Columbia Street. Judge Burke's Building (905 Second Avenue) of 1895 represents the decorative, derivative, but imaginative style of the flowery Victorian times. Pattern and ornamentation created by detailing in stone and brick produce a richness and interest not often surpassed by more recent buildings. It is believed that Fischer was the architect of this building as well as several others in the Pioneer Square area. This is the only one that has been maintained.

Across Marion Street is the Exchange Building, built in 1930 by the architectural firm of John Graham, Sr. Sharp, severe, and vertical, with ornamentation confined to areas requiring emphasis, it is an honest expression of the economical direction of its time. Ornament is skillfully stylized from nature as influenced by the European "moderne" movement. One of the highest reinforced concrete structures of its day, it is prophetic of the clean, logical architecture that followed.

The Norton Building of 1960 at Columbia Street is an elegant demonstration of contemporary curtain walls applied to a rectangular parallelepiped form. Its factory-built walls are a masterpiece of contemporary detailing. Just north, the Bank of California of the 1920's is fortunately reflected in the black glass of the Norton Building. It is completely derivative from classic architecture, attempting to borrow its qualities directly from the past without present-day reference. Even the colors and materials of the four buildings seem particularly pertinent to their respective epochs.

HOGE
BUILDING

905
2d
AVE

LOUIS

CAFE FOUNT

Victor Steinbrueck

On the site of the Territorial University stands the city's leading hostelry. The Olympic Hotel, formerly located in Pioneer Square, is the center for many conventions and social activities. Built in 1926, it was designed by architects George V. Post and Son of New York, with Bebb and Gould associated locally. The massive block square building is of good quality but appears most attractive when taken in small portions such as this entrance on Seneca Street. The hotel is a part of the environmental excellence of uptown Seattle, which is also expressed in the fine shopping area of Fifth Avenue from University to Pike streets.

Mercy G Round Children's Shop
1365 Fifth Avenue

Albert Ltd. Men's Shop
1315 Fifth Avenue

Ivar's - the Captain's Table restaurant   1429 Fifth Avenue

John Doyle Bishop Inc. ladies apparel
Fifth Avenue and Union Street

Japan
Line
Fourth Avenue
and
University St

FIFTH AVENUE FAÇADES

Perhaps the oldest of Seattle's restaurants in continuous operation is the Pittsburgh Lunch, downstairs at 602 First Avenue. The old, white-tiled floor, metal ceiling, and brown wood "café" chairs and tables provide an atmosphere appropriate to its age and clientele. Its continued existence in spite of the changing status of the district must be due, in part, to its adaptability, since it now economically accommodates both Skid Road itinerants and local office workers. Places of this sort are typical of the lower part of town which is largely associated with First Avenue. Of lower economic standing than Fifth Avenue, First Avenue is the most colorful and dramatic of Seattle streets, and its characters are cast in many roles. First Avenue is both an architectural museum and the leading theater-in-the-large in which the flavor of the city can be experienced. The shops and taverns are a vivid accent to the setting.

KENNETH
HOTEL

LOANS

V. Steinbrueck
28 June 61

1204 First Avenue

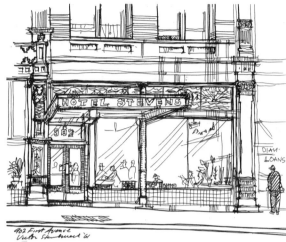

902 First Avenue
Victor Steinbrueck '61

1013 First Avenue
Victor Steinbrueck

1014 First Avenue

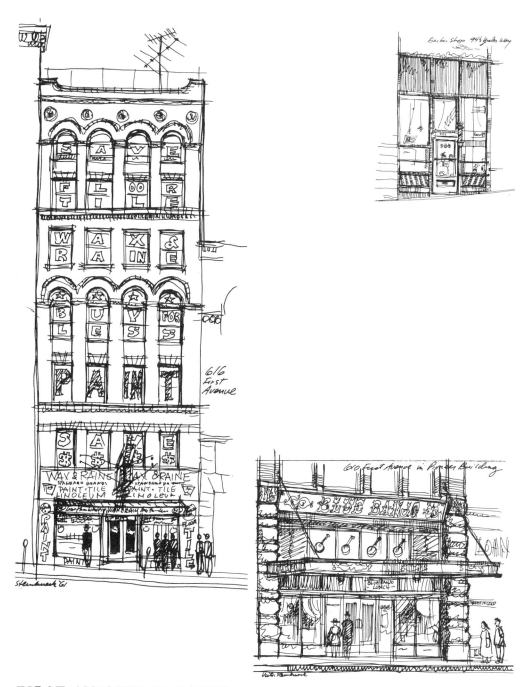

FIRST AVENUE FAÇADES

The Pike Place Market of Seattle is a particularly unique, colorful, and justly famous sight that appeals to all of the senses. It is an unusual attraction of civic value to be cherished and guarded, as well as one of the most interesting and richly picturesque shopping places in the country, and it is always worth a visit. Its charm and appeal are undeniable although difficult to identify. People of all sorts, sizes, shapes, and complexions are part of the ever changing pageant of this place both as shoppers and as merchants. Some of the nationalities that are united to form the market complex are represented in such places as a Turkish restaurant, Filipino souvenir shop, Italian grocery, Greek restaurant and beer parlor, and Japanese florist. The produce of the countryside is aggressively offered by the farmers themselves, who are mainly Japanese, Filipino, and Italian, still retaining their characteristic accents, and a number of excellent fish markets present an array of fresh sea foods. The various shops and services offer individual attention and at least the suggestion that every purchase is a bargain.

Many Seattleites, from all walks of life, are devoted to the market and are concerned regarding its obscure future, which is clouded by problems of management, inadequate parking, unsound physical structure, code restrictions, proposed "improvements," economics, and civic indifference.

The waterfront, with its docks and world commerce, holds a potential lure that has not in the past been dramatically exploited, as it has in many other cities. Now more color is being brought into the pier buildings, and some entrepreneurs, shown the way by restaurant keeper Ivar Haglund, are developing interesting and exotic restaurants and other attractions, including boatels and yacht moorages. With much municipally owned property existing along the waterfront, it is not unreasonable to hope that a water park will be developed to open the central business district to the sea. Until recently, Alaskan Way, formerly and aptly known as Railroad Avenue, has been a mundane-appearing, working waterfront, although the lure of the sea has always been present. Now its potential as a breathing space with recreational overtones is recognized as having another kind of value for the city. The old, streamlined ferryboat Kalakala suggests associations with the part that ferryboats and steamers have played and will continue to play in the growth of the Puget Sound region.

117

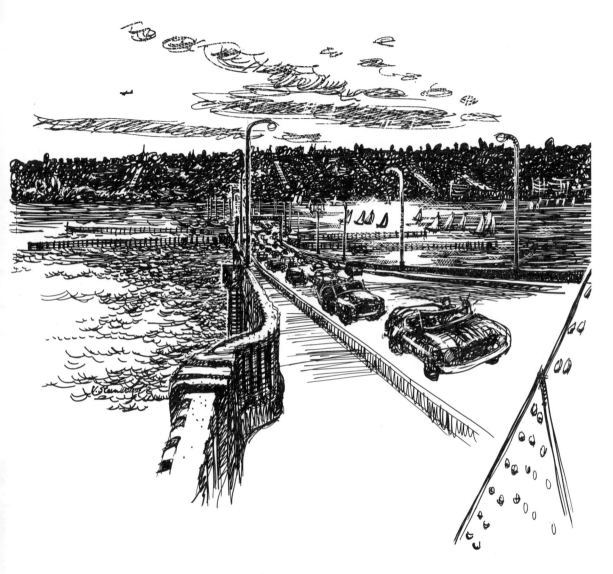

During the summer, on Tuesday and Wednesday evenings, sailboat races are held on Lake Washington by the famous Corinthian Yacht Club. Hundreds of boats participate. Sailboats are one of the few man-made objects that can compete with nature on its own terms. Crossing the Floating Bridge into the sunset while the lake is bejeweled with moving white sails is an experience that is surpassed only by actually sailing in the race. Boating, and especially sailing, is one of the great pleasures of Seattle life. The opening of a sailboat race, as seen from the Leschi Yacht Basin, shows a fleet of Six-meter sailboats crossing the starting line.

Public moorages for small boats facilitate boating and provide picturesque and colorful sights for the observer. There are several such moorages along the Lake Washington shores and at Shilshole Bay, in addition to many private moorages at Portage Bay, Lake Union, the Ship Canal, and the Duwamish Waterway. The Leschi scene shows the sailboats with their winter covers on. Two important and historic yacht clubs are the Seattle Yacht Club and the Queen City Yacht Club, both with their clubhouses and moorages at Portage Bay. Famous ocean-going sailboats are moored at the Seattle Yacht Club, which was founded in 1894 and moved to its present location in 1909.

The Hiram M. Chittenden Locks make possible the raising and lowering of vessels that pass between salt-water Puget Sound and the fresh waters of Lakes Union and Washington. Originally built to serve seagoing ships, the locks now serve thousands of small boats every week end. The smaller locks are shown with boats entering from the lower, salty side. Boats and their crews on their way to and from the many boating and fishing locations present a view of Seattle life difficult to match anywhere in the world. Water is a vital part of the city, surrounding and embracing it, while serving as a great recreational facility.

121

Driftwood-strewn beaches in the Puget Sound and San Juan Island country are available to Seattleites for week ends and longer vacations. Accessible by boat or car, they afford a ready change from city life that makes for greater enjoyment of both the country and the city.

Departing from Fauntleroy, the ferries to Vashon and Harper bring the Olympic Peninsula to Seattle's front bumper. The state-owned ferry system provides a particularly desirable means of making remote areas accessible but not overrun with automobiles.

An increasing number of trailer-borne boats has been accommodated in recent years by conveniently located small boat ramps such as this one at Shilshole Bay. Other facilities along Lake Washington and Elliott Bay are provided by the Park Department. Sport fishing for salmon and cod is a favorite pursuit of the small-boaters.

Others find a vicarious pleasure in watching the operations or visiting Fishermen's Wharf near the Ballard Bridge. Here hundreds of commercial fishermen moor their boats and work on their equipment.

STEPHIE

steinberg
1961

For those who enjoy fish but not fishing, many fresh fish markets are to be found throughout the city, such as Sam Calvo's Waterfront Fish Company market at 101 Alaskan Way. Markets like this have a special interest of their own.

Special structures developed to suit watery situations often give the water's edge a character of its own. One of the most satisfying is the Marina Mart at Westlake North and Galer streets on the west shore of Lake Union which was designed by engineer Sigmund Ivarsson in 1940. Predating the present penchant for folded roofs, the repetitious gable roofs were the best solution for sheltering the high yachts of that time. The enclosed harbor space is both interesting and harmonious. A dock-level restaurant takes advantage of the colorful boat scene and is accessible by water.

127

Another maritime structure within the city is the Alki Point Lighthouse. Although there is another at West Point, west of Shilshole Bay, it is still unusual to find such structures within a city. A visitor to the lighthouse, turning his back on the city, is struck with an overwhelming feeling of the sea and of the remoteness of distant places. Visiting hours are scheduled.

Houseboats are houses rather than boats, but they do float, usually on cedar logs or sealed oil barrels. People live in them because they don't have to mow the water. The pleasant, bohemian way of life enjoyed by houseboat colonies on Lake Union and Portage Bay is gradually being exterminated by various forms of "progress," such as bridges, apartments, marinas, building codes, and city officials. Very few of these unique homes are well designed or even designed, but the nature of their situation forces upon them restrictions that produce a certain picturesque harmony.

2203 Fairview Avenue North
on Lake Union

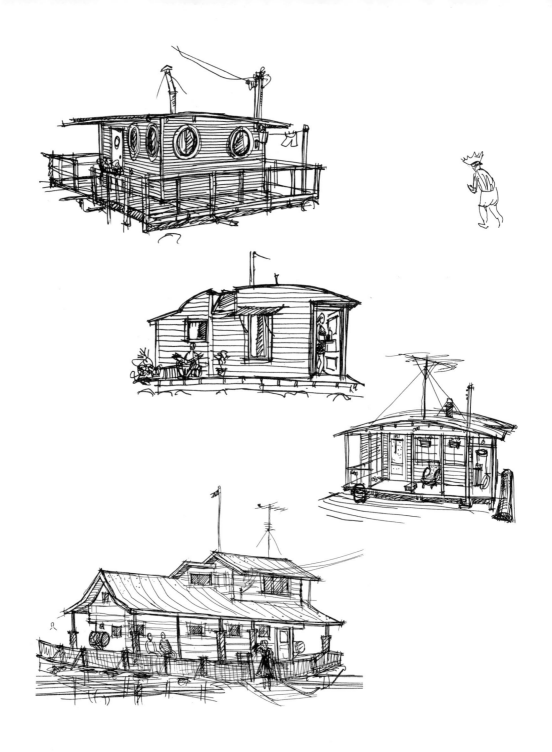

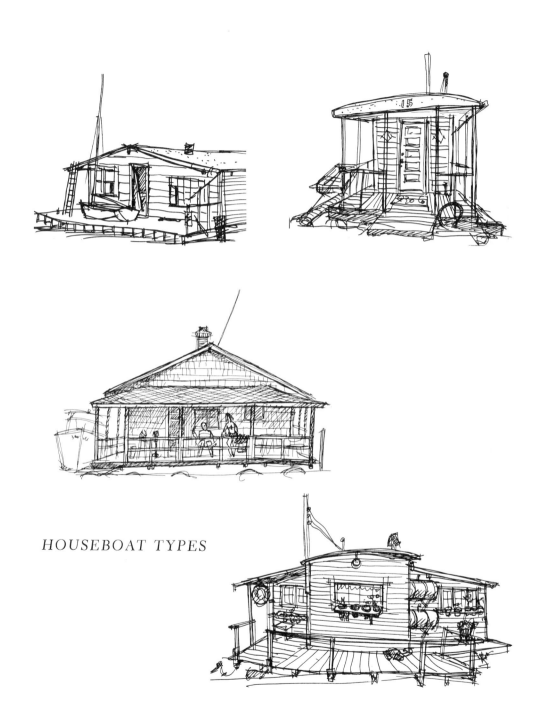

HOUSEBOAT TYPES

131

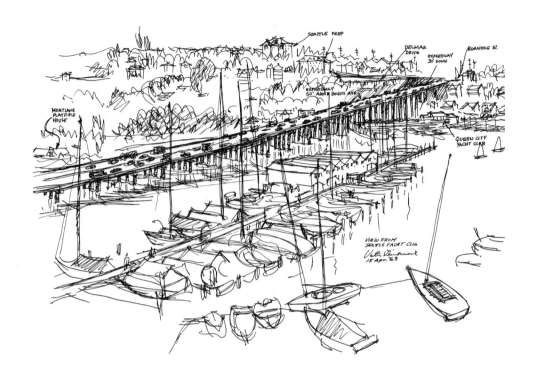

Persons who care about the city have been concerned over the ruthless transgressions and the lack of esthetic quality of new constructions such as the costly freeway and the Portage Bay–Arboretum–Evergreen Point Bridge Expressway. Marvelous natural settings are being violated by the naked brutality of unimaginative structures such as this proposed crossing of Portage Bay, which eliminates fifty houseboats while casting its shadow and noise across the tranquil boat haven. Citizen protests, if heeded, may alter the severity of the outrage. If the city is to be rebuilt for the automobile alone, there will be no place for the people.

Landlocked Green Lake is a fortunately located recreational center and breathing space within a large residential area. The lake is available to all, and much of the city enjoys its two bathing beaches, its fishing for the young and hopeful, and the cycling path that encircles it. Other activities include boat racing and Fourth of July fireworks.

Two really great city parks are Lincoln and Seward. Lincoln Park looks out over Puget Sound from a bluff near Fauntleroy. Evergreens identify the area as particularly Northwest. A fine natural peninsula projecting into Lake Washington is occupied entirely by Seward Park. Picnic shelters are well used, as in this sketch showing neighborhood ladies playing bridge while their children romp nearby. These large parks have tremendous value to the city as readily accessible relief from streets and buildings.

The University of Washington Arboretum, originally laid out by the Olmstead Brothers, landscape architects, is another green interlude in the city's pattern. With its outstanding and extensive botanical collection, it serves a particular purpose among Seattle parks and is very dear to the hearts of many citizens. One group, the Arboretum Foundation, is completely devoted to its development and good use. A leisurely drive on the boulevard through the bower of oak trees is a most enjoyable experience in motion. Walks through the Arboretum hold many pleasures as the foliage changes with the seasons. This area has been one of the city's most precious assets, exemplifying the quality of landscape possible here.

135

Through the loving care and infinite skill of landscape architect Juki Iida of Tokyo, and the generosity of some local citizens, the city has acquired a delightful Japanese garden and teahouse in the Arboretum. Since its opening in 1960, it has been enjoyed by hundreds of visitors daily. The three-acre garden of plants, rocks, and water is the largest of its kind in America. Mr. Iida personally supervised every aspect of the planning and construction.

A residential neighborhood breathing space of fitting size and unpretentious character is the small park with waiting shelter at Denny Blaine. The charming structure shows some of the qualities of architect Ellsworth Storey's work which have come to be appreciated. There is a pleasing combination of heavy fieldstones, natural wood poles used as structure, and nice shingle work, producing a comfortable and friendly space of refined naturalness. Nearby trees and a circular lily pond add to the feeling of simple serenity and repose, and the entire district is enriched by this pleasant accommodation.

Nature's kindness to man is demonstrated by such streets as Bigelow Avenue on Queen Anne Hill, where the residential street becomes a boulevard with trees dominating the scene. With the lush green shelter of these trees creating variations of sunlight and shadow, the architectural features become relatively unimportant, and the street assumes a quality far more enjoyable than would be possible on a naked street.

Formerly a tree-lined drive, Ravenna Boulevard south of Green Lake is crossed by massive freeway structures. The boulevard is brought to a dead stop visually at the crossing, and a pleasant experience in motion is destroyed. Many persons have expressed concern over the seemingly ruthless brutality of the encroachment of these structures upon the community.

Back in 1912, a precedent for good design in civic construction was established by the work of Willcox and Sayward, architects, in designing the retaining walls along Queen Anne Boulevard at Eighth Place West and West Lee Street. W. R. B. Willcox later became the dean of the College of Architecture and Allied Arts at the University of Oregon.

TOO BAD
ABOUT
THESE POLES →

STAY
IN ONE
LANE

Victor Steinbrueck 1961
TUNNEL PORTALS
LAKE WASHINGTON FLOATING BRIDGE

Few cities have an entrance equal to this beautiful, sculptured tunnel portal at the west side of the Lake Washington Floating Bridge. Architect Lloyd Lovegren was on the staff of the State Highway Department and participated in the design with the engineers. The large, concrete, low-relief sculptures were the result of further collaboration by Lovegren with artist James FitzGerald. Civic pride is increased by the esthetic satisfaction that this excellent public structure has given to passing motorists ever since it was built in 1940.

An unusual reminder of the past is the active truck farm of the Picardo family at Twenty-seventh Avenue Northeast and Northeast Seventy-eighth Street, occupying several acres within a typical middle-class residential neighborhood. As it stands, it provides a fruitful experience for the neighborhood children while yielding contrasts of space and architecture. The old barn is a simple example of the anonymous architecture that has always been part of the local scene. The possible influence of such buildings on architecture has not been fully considered although architects are often aware of their qualities. Attempts are being made to have the farm rezoned as other than residential in order to gain economic advantages.

Woodland Park with its many popular attractions is probably the most used and best known of the city's parks. An extensive and varied zoo attracts an extensive and varied group of people. Which is more interesting depends on one's point of view. The children's playland competes for the attention and dimes of the young citizen. The picnic shelters and stoves are one of the well-used centers for the fulfillment of the well-established Seattle institution of picnicking. Fair weather presents innumerable occasions for picnics, and the public parks and countryside provide the settings.

143

Inhabitants of the Skid Road and of lower downtown find some comfort on a warm summer's eve by taking advantage of the open, green lawn at City Hall Park immediately south of the County-City Building. Other city dwellers in the central area find the next available green space at Denny Park in the Regrade district. Hope continues that this space will be made more livable and that other open spaces will appear in the downtown area through the graces of our city fathers and the efforts of the citizenry.

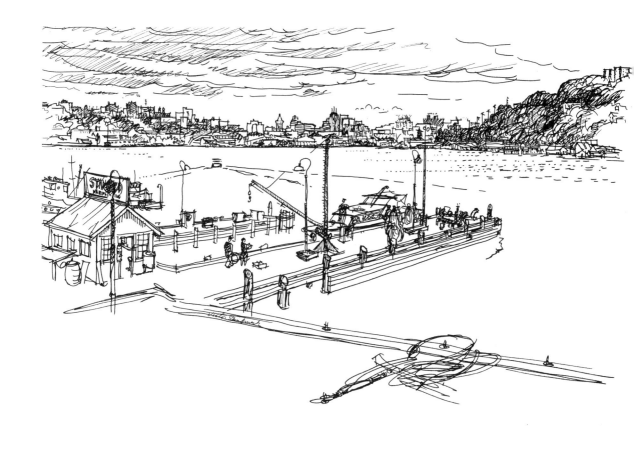

The flame-, cinder-, and odor-belching gas plant on a promontory at the north shore of Lake Union has been a spectacular landmark for years, especially with the blinking "Grandma's Cookies" sign just behind it. Now that the plant is to be eliminated through the piping in of natural gas, this location will become available for other uses. It is hoped that it will be acquired as a special kind of park. An urban park accessible by boat has been proposed. The sunny southern exposure suggests an all-season park, taking advantage of the fine view of the central business district, and the barren terrain offers an opportunity for the development of cultural facilities less suitable to the outlying natural parks.

Descendants of Seattle's (or Duwamps') earliest families take shelter on a hot day under the 1911-vintage iron pergola at Pioneer Square. Because their white brothers have not opened their hearts to them elsewhere, the Indians find that this area serves as a gathering place—as it was in the beginning. An Indian center located at 2604 First Avenue operates as a base for more productive activities.

Pioneer Square's rich association with the past provides a fitting place to recall a portion of Chief Seattle's eloquent speech to Territorial Governor Isaac I. Stevens in 1854: "Every part of this country is sacred to my people. Every hillside, every valley, every plain and grove has been hallowed by some fond memory or some sad experience of my tribe. And when the last Red Man shall have perished from the earth and his memory among the white men shall have become a myth, these shores will swim with the invisible dead of my tribe, and when your children's children shall think themselves alone in the fields, the store, the shop, upon the highway or in the silence of the pathless woods, they will not be alone. In all the earth, there is no place dedicated to solitude. At night when the streets of your cities and villages will be silent and you think them deserted, they will throng with the returning hosts that once filled and still love this beautiful land. The white man will never be alone. Let him be just and deal kindly with my people, for the dead are not powerless. Dead, did I say? There is no death—only a change of worlds."

Architecture and Building

The experience of architecture is almost always with us. City people are usually either within architecture or on their way to or from a piece of architecture. The man-made environment of our cities, whether for better or for worse, is largely determined by architecture and by the urban spaces formed by groups of architectural units. Architects apply their talents toward producing individual buildings of unique and special quality. The Puget Sound area is renowned for the generally excellent quality of architecturally designed residences, small buildings, and schools, and there are many examples of these achievements, some of which have been selected for illustration.

In spite of the number of good architects available, however, considerable construction takes place without the direct and full benefit of architectural talents. Other forces tend very strongly to shape our buildings. These include financial interests, lay owners and boards, governmental agencies, building and zoning regulations, and other elements not necessarily noted for awareness of cultural or esthetic values. The dominance of these forces is responsible for the broad mass of mediocre building in America today, as contrasted with architecture of quality. The opposite extreme is the "high-style" architecture that may be the result of an apparently brilliant but unrealistic approach not appropriate to the environment or the purpose but tending to ignore or overrule such considerations. Neither of these directions is ideal, although the individual architect striving to produce an architectural masterpiece may make an influential contribution to the environment.

The situation can be improved only through broader cultural awareness and appreciation of the importance and value of creative architecture and through total planning with the democratic involvement of all concerned. Architecture cannot rise far above the social, economic, and technical considerations that produce it—nor should it. But building that does not respect the higher social and cultural values and goals does permanent injury to the city and to all its inhabitants, since none can escape it. A concern for place and a respect for existing qualities are necessary. He who builds a building is also building a city.

Examples illustrated have been selected to show the trend of Seattle architecture of quality through the years, as well as some of the characteristic residences that are more properly considered "building" rather than "architecture." Although a committee of architects of the Seattle Chapter of the American Institute of Architects selected a representative list of architecture, both old and new, which is included in the group illustrated, the items actually chosen are the result of the author's personal prejudices, idiosyncrasies, and convenience—perhaps more obviously than he, himself, realizes. There are some glaring omissions, not to be taken as a reflection upon any work not included. This is not a comprehensive guide either to architecture or to Seattle.

Awareness of the physical environment, including architecture, is the first requirement for developing a more beautiful city worthy of its setting and its people. Respect for environment or place as well as for all people is a necessity for the creation of a truly great Seattle.

Since many of the illustrations are private residences it is requested that observers respect the privacy of the owners.

ONE OF A ROW OF VICTORIAN HOUSES
23 & E MARION — C 1892

The pattern of change in ordinary homes produced by speculative builders over a period of seventy years is well illustrated in our neighborhoods. Along with slowly changing technology and methods, reflections of social attitudes are demonstrated. On the east side of Twenty-third Avenue at East Marion Street is a row of almost identical houses built about 1892. They are amusing remnants of Victorian extravagance and confidence. Decorative woodwork was available as stock items, often incorporated according to the skill and imagination of carpenters. The parlor, dining room, and kitchen were downstairs, with sleeping quarters upstairs. Toilets were beginning to be moved inside.

151

Frills of Victorian times gave way to a more natural kind of bungalow or cottage style in the 1910 decade. With lower pitched wide roofs and porches, these houses often included extra rooms in the attic. Beamed and bracketed construction, often false but not noticeably so, combined with natural shingle and wood siding to produce unpretentious homes consistent with the climate. These still seem appropriate today. The main floor was usually raised to allow direct windows into the basement and to avoid excessive concrete work. Terraced yards above the streets are peculiar not to this time but to Seattle's hilly terrain. Brooklyn Avenue Northeast near Northeast Sixty-fourth Street is the location of this group.

With increased worldliness and prosperity, the 1920's produced homes such as these along Fifteenth Avenue South near South Hanford Street on Beacon Hill. There were more innovations made in the forms of mass and roof although details were of established stock patterns. Bungalows continued, with the second story or half story often included in an almost too clever fashion. Basement garages at the front of the house were often made possible by the raised ground as in this sketch. Colors were usually white or pastel. Brick veneer houses were also popular, falsely implying a quality superior to that of wood.

153

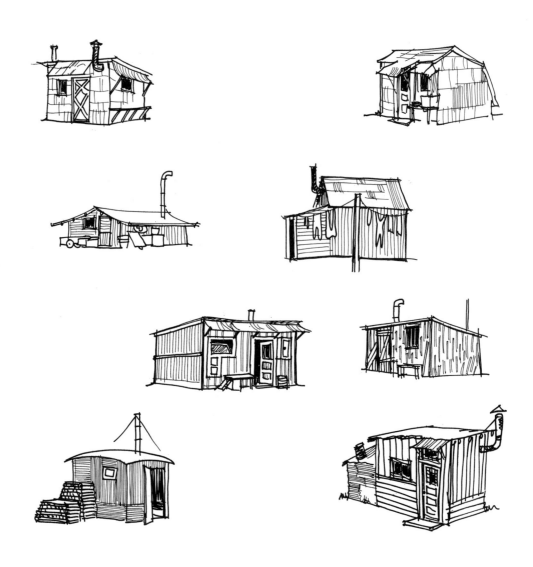

During the 1930's there was little building although examples can be found of economical, close-cropped homes that can be characterized as both severe and "cute." Another sort of home, no longer extant, expressed the economics of the times, often relating in basic concept to more worldly structures. These were the homes of the unemployed in the several "Hoovervilles" in Seattle's industrial areas. The sketches were made in 1933.

Some of the nicer developments of the 1940 decade involved architectural firms in the architecture, with stock plans tailored to suit each lot and to produce variety. In a few situations, the tracts were tremendously enhanced by the saving of some of the existing trees, as in the Wedgewood district at Thirty-fifth Avenue Northeast and Northeast Eighty-first Street. Masonry, when used, was likely to be merely a decorative element.

Typical for the smaller speculative builder in the last decade is the solid brick-veneered, asphalt-shingled, hip-roofed, one-story house. The identifying elements of these examples of sagacious investment are planter boxes, small porches, stock wrought-iron railings, concrete barbecue patios, aluminum sash, nursery specimen landscaping, flowered rockery retaining walls, and television antennas reaching into outer space.

During the 1950's, independent architects participated in several speculative developments. This one, by architects Bassetti and Morse and builder Theo Caldwell, demonstrates a straightforward approach to planning pleasing and economical small homes together in a natural setting. Within the limitations of a small development, a consistent contemporary neighborhood resulted as seen from the George Gulacsik residence at 1700 Ninety-ninth Northeast in Bellevue. Similar houses were combined at West Mercer Way near Southeast Forty-third Street on Mercer Island. The Surrey Downs tract in Bellevue by architects Mithun and Nesland is another contemporary residential development of quality by speculative builders.

Eastgate
Eastgate Drive & 148 S.E.

Lake Hills
157 S.E. & S.E. 4th

Massive speculative developments of hundreds of homes have taken place in Seattle's suburbia to the north, east, and south in recent years. The design quality of homes and properties is in advance of most developments in older parts of the county. Values have appeared to be high and financing easy, although problems have arisen as a result of lack of consideration for community facilities, and county planning efforts have been taxed to the utmost. Land speculation has proved exceedingly profitable as tracts continue to appear. Homogeneous neighborhoods such as Lake Hills (above) and Eastgate (below) continue to be typical. There is a freshness and excitement to these developments, partly because of the prolific young families that are attracted to them.

In 1941, Seattle's first federally sponsored slum clearance low-income housing project was built on "Profanity Hill" at Yesler Way and Broadway. Each family unit has its own private sitting-out area and yard and is afforded a view by the terrace site planning and flat shed roofs. The design and color of the well-arranged buildings, with their nicely maintained gardens, make this good contemporary architecture. Only in such a public project has it been possible to provide play areas and community social and recreational facilities giving a most complete environment. Architects William Aitken, William J. Bain, John T. Jacobsen, J. Lister Holmes, and George W. Stoddard combined to produce this project.

Seattle is proud of the maintenance and operation of its public housing projects, such as the Holly Park Housing Project on Beacon Hill, which have fitted so well into the various communities. This was built in 1943 by architects John Paul Jones, Fred Ahlson, and Paul Thiry. There is a low-density, suburban quality to the freely located two- and four-unit apartments, with plenty of space for play yards and community facilities. The individual units are of simple but excellent design that looks as handsome today as when they were built. The community building is particularly appropriate.

159

In 1903, the young architect Ellsworth Storey moved to Seattle from Illinois and built these two homes at 260 and 270 Dorffel Drive East, one for his bride and himself, one for his parents. Architects have admired the houses ever since for their originality, enduring quality, and appropriateness to the region. Decorative but simply shaped woodwork contrasts with brown shingle siding and skillfully related wide roof shapes to produce architecture of unassuming quality and integrity which is closely related to the best work of today.

COTTAGES AT COLMAN PARK
ELLSWORTH STOREY - ARCHITECT - 1915

Ten years later, Storey built a series of small cottages at Colman Park in order to provide "low rental in a good neighborhood." These homes are an excellent example of charming design and fine detailing in a contemporary manner far in advance of its time. There is a fitting, almost indigenous quality in their simple wooden forms as they appear to ramble up the wooded hillside.

The Heffernan house is now used as a teachers' residence for the Helen Bush Parkside School, and the large garage has been adapted to serve as kindergarten. Cutter and Malmgren were the architects who produced this refined mansion in the first decade of the century. Derivative from English Tudor architecture, it is refined in detail and workmanship. Particularly elegant are the barge boards at the roof's edge of carved open woodwork. The house is located at 408 Lake Washington Boulevard East.

Architect Andrew Willatsen had worked for Frank Lloyd Wright before coming to Seattle to produce courageous architecture in the Wright manner, which, with its organic quality, strongly expressed roof planes, and definite patterns, appeared most fitting to this region. Most other architects at that time were working in traditional styles. This house was built in 1913 at 2021 East Lynn Street in the Montlake district.

Refined and elegant domestic architecture was produced by architect Arthur Loveless during his many years of practice. The Corbett house at 300 Maiden Lane East is typical of his work in the English manner done during the 1920's.

A pleasant example of quality architecture in the traditional manner is the Norman-style residence at 128 Lake Washington Boulevard East, built for Mr. and Mrs. Arthur J. Krauss in 1928 by architect Carl F. Gould, Sr. Olmstead Brothers were the landscape architects who planned the informal development of the sloping site with its private beach on the lake shore. There are other fine, large homes in the general area and in Madison Park and Laurelhurst, as well as in the exclusive, restricted districts such as Broadmoor and The Highlands.

The well-known architect Paul Thiry is one of the pillars of the contemporary movement. His own house at 330 Thirty-fifth Avenue East, built in 1936, illustrates the ·clean, direct approach associated with the International Style, which placed the creative responsibility upon the designer rather than upon the past.

Artist Ambrose Patterson commissioned the young progressive architect John R. Sproule to produce this modern residence in 1936. Somewhat similar in character to the International Style, it is an imaginative and skillful composition of forms not derivative from other works. The location is 3927 Belvoir Place Northeast.

During the late 1930's, another young architect of creative strength and ability, who became a forerunner in the development of honest and appropriate local architecture, was John T. Jacobsen. The red-stained wooden house of the Andrew Gunbys at 1118 East Roanoke Street is piquant and charming in its directness. Scandinavian influence can be recognized and appreciated.

One of the most imaginative and inspirational architects in the Northwest is former Professor Lionel Pries, whose own home is an eloquent manifestation of his unique talents. The lush planting helps to amplify the charm of the place, which cannot be related to any one particular era. The location is 3132 West Laurelhurst Drive Northeast.

The Preston house at 745 McGilvra Boulevard East is one of the fine homes produced by architects Terry, Tucker, and Shields in the early 1950's. With their native woods and simple, gable-roofed forms, these houses fit gracefully into the varied hillside sites. Washington Park is one of the fine, older residential districts.

West Mercer Way on Mercer Island is a showcase of well-designed residential architecture. One of the most pleasing is the home of Dr. and Mrs. Cyrus Rubin at 6105 Southeast Thirty-second Street, designed by architects Ibsen Nelsen and Russell Sabin. It is a thoughtful and personal style of home, pleasantly landscaped, which speaks well for both architect and client.

Hilltop Community is a contemporary development suited to its fine setting. Commanding sweeping panoramas from its lofty hilltop south of Eastgate, it is a controlled community with a variety of interesting and original residences that show the fine work of talented architects. An excellent example has been established here for others to follow. One of the pleasantest homes in the region is that of architect Perry B. Johanson, with its sprawling architecture set in an enjoyable landscape with magnificent views.

A carefully planned and detailed small home in a simple form is the Alden Mason house at 2545 Boyer Avenue, built in 1952. Wood is used interestingly and directly with a concrete masonry and glass block foundation. The architect is Victor Steinbrueck.

An example of architecture done with technical excellence and perfection, but with restraint of form appropriate to a small home, is Mrs. Mary-Jane Worth's residence by architect Wendell Lovett. The basic architectural philosophy expressed emphasizes the man-made quality of the architecture rather than an organic quality of growing out of the site. The location is 4218 Northeast Ninety-second Street.

Architect Paul Hayden Kirk designed this excellent contemporary wooden house, located in the woods at 4157 West Mercer Way, for his brother, Blair Kirk. It shows masterful spatial design and composition, and fine knowledge of wood construction as a design consideration, while confidently making the best of a natural setting.

166

A woodsy house that seems to grow right out of the Puget Sound country is this small house in Richmond Highlands designed for the Bill Holm family by architect Gene Zema in 1960. The sloping site with its view of Puget Sound has been left in its natural state and is rich in native growth. The steep-pitched roof and direct use of wood are particularly appropriate. Bill Holm is an artist skilled in the arts of the local Indians, and his home achieves a personal quality by reflecting this interest.

Architect Kirtland Cutter designed the Rainier Club in 1904, but it has been worked over by several architects since then. The club, founded in 1888, is the city's oldest. The stalwart dignity of its ivy-colored, Germanic town house character contrasts quaintly with the contemporary urban setting and emphasizes the prestige and exclusiveness of the group.

In 1908, the Seattle Golf and Country Club moved out to this building in the Highlands which was planned by architects Cutter and Malmgren under the supervision of Andrew Willatsen. The style, which utilizes dark brown wood siding and detail in contrast with white stucco, is derivative from the mountain architecture of Central Europe. The building, however, needs no apology for its appropriateness and originality at a time when less creative architecture was being copied from traditional sources. The wide, shingled roofs on bracketed beams are decorative and fitting to the material and the climate.

The shopping and apartment group designed and built by architect Arthur L. Love-less in 1931 is architecture of enduring quality. While the style is derivative from the English, it is handled with a fresh and creative approach that has produced a charming building. There is a spatial lesson in the personal quality of the architecture and its pleasant interior court. The location is 711 Broadway East.

The Northeast Branch Public Library, built in 1954 by architect Paul Thiry, is a prototype for handsome neighborhood libraries. Steel construction in a residential idiom, with considerable restraint and confidence expressed in the simple shape, produced a building of lasting quality. It is located at 6801 Thirty-fifth Avenue Northeast.

PAUL KIRKS OFFICE BUILDING
FAIRVIEW & E NEWTON

Architect Paul Hayden Kirk's small office building at Fairview Avenue North and Newton Street is a fine example of the personal quality of this firm's work. A handsome and elegant architecture has been created through the use of adroitly detailed wood, both structurally and as surface pattern. All exposed wood is stained dark brown, with a touch of brightness added in brilliantly colored glass vent louvers along the corridor.

An excellent small office building at 330 Fairview Avenue North was built by architects Waldron and Dietz in 1959. Skillful planning placed the building over its parking area, dramatized the stairway and ramp, and produced uncluttered development of the office areas. The result is a clean, sharp, and restrained form of stucco and glass.

The Allison Apartments at 4329 Fifteenth Avenue South have a charming quality created by harmoniously patterned brown wood and white stucco. Consistent and confident detailing of the woodwork and pleasant landscaping are part of this quality. A. O. Bumgardner and Partners were the architects for the apartments, which were built in 1959.

Architects Bassetti and Morse have developed a pleasantly spaced group of walk-up apartments for staff housing for the University Hospital at University Way Northeast and Northeast Pacific Street. In contrast to less personal high-rise housing, a situation is created where social contacts and relationships are encouraged by the environment. The use of wood exteriors and idiomatic gable roofs is consistent with the nature of the project, which is not yet totally completed.

171

The Blakeley Psychiatric Group Clinic at 2271 Northeast Fifty-first Street, built by architect Paul Hayden Kirk in 1956, demonstrates the skill of the architect in creating a most pleasant and appropriate atmosphere through imaginative use of color, materials, and architectural spaces.

Sympathetic collaboration between an understanding owner and a talented architect produced an imaginative and stimulating building in 1960 for the publishing and printing plant of Pacific Builder and Engineers, Inc. A concrete hyperbolic paraboloid roof and structure combined with natural stained wood, on a difficult site at 1945 Yale Place North, result in a nicely composed expression of Seattle's contemporary architecture. A. O. Bumgardner and Partners were the architects.

The Sodergren Apartments at 3767 University Way Northeast were designed by architect Ralph Anderson in 1956. Thoughtful use of wood construction sensitively detailed throughout adds charm to this four-unit apartment, which is very much in the tradition of the region. The entire exterior is stained khaki color.

Architects Terry, Tucker, and Shields built this architectural office for themselves in 1946 of decoratively combined split cedar siding and rough Wilkeson sandstone masonry. Landscape handled in a natural way adds to the dignified but interesting quality of the architecture. It is located at 914 Lakeview Boulevard East.

Built in 1960, the Faculty Center Building at the University of Washington is fortunately situated to enjoy a sweeping panorama of Union Bay, Lake Washington, and the Cascade Range. All the architecture had to do was respect the site and the fine trees already there while providing a variety of necessary spaces. White stucco, glass, and gray steel, with native wood interiors, and a conscious use of space itself as a design element were the means employed to produce a pleasantly scaled environment by architects Paul Hayden Kirk and Associates and Victor Steinbrueck.

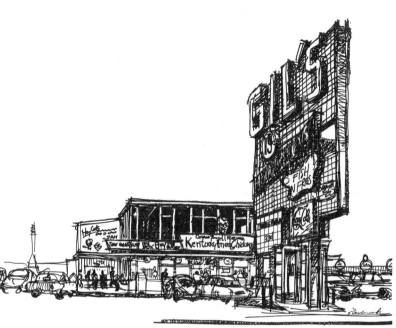

The monumental sign proclaiming "Gil's 19¢ Hamburgers" is an unavoidable attraction for anyone in the area of Rainier Avenue South and South Genesee Street. There is an almost sculptural quality to the massive steel structure in front of the bedecked glass drive-in hamburger factory which suggests that perhaps here is the 19¢ Le Corbusier, too. This is contemporary American building, not particularly local in character. Koby's Fish and Chips at Leschi contrasts with Gil's both in size and in aggressiveness. Specializing in fish and chips through the summer months, the proprietor includes friendliness and a smile with every order. The completely anonymous building, with the rustic yard furniture outside for viewing water activities, is a part of the Seattle scene.

American supermarkets present a type of superarchitecture particularly American and completely contemporary in every respect. Foreign visitors marvel at both the clean architecture and the impressive displays of foods and many other products. Even a well-designed building like the Tradewell Store at Empire Way South in the Holly Park shopping area, however, is killed by the sea of asphalt and automobiles surrounding it, not to mention the distraction of the overhead utility elements. Planners, architects, and merchants must realize the value of a pleasant environment for shopping and plan marketing places for people, not for automobiles.

South from Queen Anne Hill is a broad view of the site of the World's Fair and future Seattle Center, with the central business district beyond. Many of the buildings were designed by local architects, with Paul Thiry being responsible for site planning and the State Coliseum, as well as several lesser buildings. The site was planned around the existing Civic Auditorium, Armory, and High School Memorial Stadium; the auditorium has been remodeled to become the Opera House by architects Chiarelli and Priteca. Cultural facilities are the Playhouse and Exhibition Hall by Kirk, Wallace, and McKinley.

Privately owned on property acquired from the city, the Space Needle symbolically and actually dominates the architectural complex because of its monumental verticality. Its restaurant and observation tower are expected to be a permanent and profitable addition to Seattle. The Federal Science Building, providing a dignified and conservative contrast with more flamboyant and less studied promotional architecture, symbolizes the conservatism of bureaucratic governmental attitudes. Its future use as part of the permanent Seattle Center is still undecided. The dazzling white courtyard is a most dramatic setting.

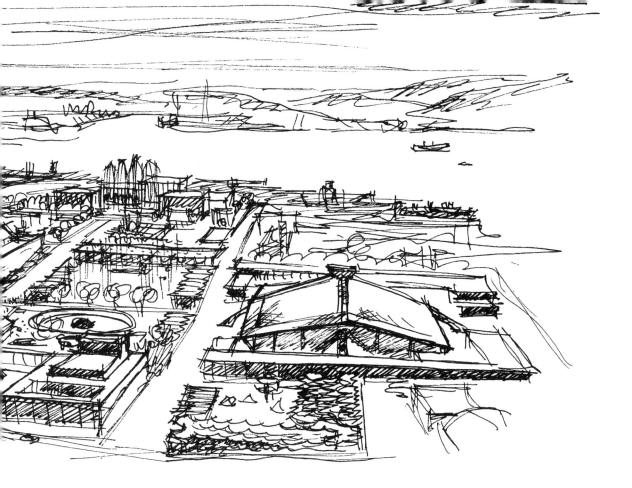

The development of the Seattle Center,
containing many permanent buildings,
presents a challenging possibility as a focus
for yet unidentified activities. It is hoped
that the cultural life of the city will be enhanced in proportion to the effort involved
in producing the center. The situation is
enriched by many excellent permanent
works of art, including the large central
fountain, that have been incorporated into
the buildings and the site. The temporary
population explosion produced during
the fair calls attention to the vital need for
thorough and competent total planning
for the growing city of the future.

A revealing contrast is demonstrated by viewing the Federal Science Building from the outside at Denny Way and Fourth Avenue and from inside the Seattle Center grounds. Architect Minoru Yamasaki, associated with architects Naramore, Bain, Brady, and Johanson, created an abstract Gothic inner court of crystalline quality contrasting both with the outer urban world and with the architecture of the Seattle World's Fair. The outside view is typical of the unpleasant urban clutter in every American city which dominates both architecture and cityscape, although this scene is changing because of the fair. The inner view reveals Yamasaki's skill in providing an elegant oasis that separates his carefully studied architecture from the less precious outer world.

St. Joseph Church was built in 1932 of reinforced exposed concrete, both exterior and interior, with a minimum of exterior cast stone ornament and painted interior decoration. A more costly, traditional design had been begun but fortunately was discarded because of the economic depression, and the work was given to architects A. H. Albertson and Associates with Joseph Wilson as the designer. A lastingly beautiful building resulted, with the design achieving a warmth and spiritual quality far transcending its apparently severe material as it forms a background for the traditional Catholic service. The location is 732 Eighteenth Avenue East.

Architect Ellsworth Storey designed the chapel and rectory of the Episcopal Church of the Epiphany, which were built near Denny Blaine Lake Park in 1911. The buildings, eclectic in style, are derivative from English Tudor architecture, but creative originality is demonstrated in the carefully detailed wooden forms, which are combined to achieve a pleasantly intimate quality that has stood the test of time.

An original contemporary church group of excellent quality, appropriate to the region and to this time, is the Bellevue Presbyterian Church at 1720 100th Avenue Northeast in Bellevue. The A-frame church structure is composed harmoniously with flat-roofed educational and social elements, using natural wood and stone in a pleasantly landscaped setting. Architects are Mithun, Ridenour, and Cochran.

St. Elizabeth's Episcopal Church, produced by architects Durham, Anderson, and Freed in 1958, is located at 1005 Southwest 152nd Street in Lake Burien. The arched nave and sanctuary are fittingly elevating and impressive both in exterior and interior. The use of wood to achieve the symbolic and dramatic form is most effective.

Temple de Hirsch at Sixteenth Avenue and East Pike Street, built in 1960, is a dramatic symbol of its religion. The work of several artists is incorporated into the spectacular cast stone edifice designed by John Detlie in association with architect B. Marcus Priteca.

Unity Church at 200 Eighth Avenue North presents an interesting contrast between the graceful circular chapel and the severe adjoining two-story educational building. Young, Richardson, and Carleton were the architects for the church, built in 1960.

Architects Grant, Copeland, Chervenak, and Associates designed the Eastgate Lutheran Church of Christ the King in 1956. It is located at Eastgate Drive and 148th Avenue Southeast. The unsymmetrical wooden structure gracefully accents and dominates a sloping hillside above the shopping center of suburban Eastgate. In size and detail, it blends appropriately with the nearby homes, while adding an appealingly fresh design quality.

The Catholic Church of Saint George at 5300 Thirteenth Avenue South, built in 1954, is a concrete structure of simple dignity, typical of the work of architect Paul Thiry.

Architects Gotteland and Kocarski designed the Catholic Church of Our Lady of the Lake at 8900 Thirty-fifth Avenue Northeast to harmonize with the adjoining school group, which is the work of architect Paul Thiry. A charming chapel by Thiry was removed to make way for the monumental red brick church and its contrasting white concrete tower in 1960.

One of the most attractively picturesque buildings in the Seattle area is the small
Russian-American Orthodox Cathedral of Saint Spiridon at Yale Avenue North and
Harrison Street. The many blue cupolas with golden crosses are typically Russian.
The congregation was founded in 1895, and this church was erected in 1936 with
Ivan Palmaw as the architect. It symbolizes the variety of national groups who par-
ticipate in the life of the city while still maintaining respect for their origins.

This simple scene along the edge of Union Bay, which was formerly a wildlife sanctuary, no longer exists since it was destroyed to make way for new expressway construction. The passing of this enjoyable section of cherished wilderness within the city is symbolic of the ruthless brutality of many esthetic crimes perpetrated in the name of improvement and progress. If its loss is not allowed to go unheeded or without sorrow, there is hope that this may be the last of such acts which ignore the setting, the place, and the people who are to be served. Respect for our environment and recognition of the obligation to enhance it for the enjoyment of all people are vital if Seattle is to become a great city. The potential exists without a doubt, so it is fitting that the goals of broad cultural education and understanding which can be achieved through our public school system be given recognition by the sketches of the schools in the following pages. Our homes and our schools are the environment for shaping the future.

The town of Georgetown had already built this two-and-a-half-story grade school before its annexation to Seattle in 1910. High classrooms with narrow windows "punched" into wooden walls contrast with present-day one-story school buildings and their continuous strip windows. There are many such buildings in Seattle, usually at least one in each of the older neighborhoods. Many Seattleites have a sentimental attachment for these places of learning. The architecture is extremely unpretentious and without conscious style, but not without merit.

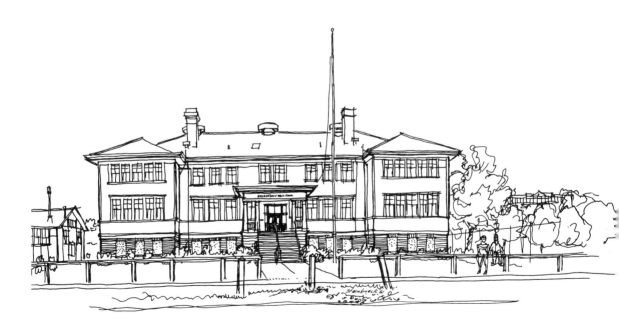

The Harrison Elementary School is the
result of the enlargement of an inadequate
older facility in 1956 by architects Jones
and Bindon. An unostentatious, straightforward design of lasting quality, still consistent with present-day contemporary
architecture, it provides a pleasant atmosphere for teaching in an unusually mixed
economic and racial neighborhood.

Expanding, suburban Edmonds has been
accommodating its growing population
with many new schools of excellent and
progressive design demonstrating thoughtful consideration of the importance of
suitable educational environment for children. One of the pleasantest is illustrated
in this view of the covered play area and
one of the many semienclosed courts of
the Westgate Elementary School, built
by architect Dan Miller in 1959. Limited
use of primary colors accents the comfortable and varied outdoor spaces.

Roosevelt High School, built in 1922 by the architectural firm of Floyd Naramore, is one of the city's outstanding high schools scholastically. The architecture, while not unusual, is commendable for its restraint and regularity of form and pattern in brick and terra cotta. It is typical of the era from the 1920's through the second World War.

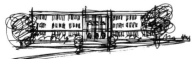

The Catherine Blaine Junior High School, at 2550 Thirty-fourth Avenue West, is an outstanding complete school that also provides social facilities in conjunction with the Seattle Park Board on a nineteen-acre site. The classrooms rely mainly on natural lighting through sawtooth skylights and antiglare ceiling baffles, with a visual window strip. The unit in the foreground is for music practice. The school was built in 1952 by architects J. Lister Holmes and Associates, Robert Dietz, and Charles MacDonald.

Architects Naramore, Bain, Brady, and Johanson created the Edward S. Ingraham High School in 1960 at North 135th Street and Wallingford Avenue North. It is a pleasing and competent educational group of lasting quality. The varied forms of the gymnasiums and auditorium units contrast with the long blocks of classroom wings.

Architect Ralph Burkhard designed the Mountlake Terrace High School, built in 1960, which is grouped around a very dramatic central landscaped court. Concrete and colorful plastic are used to produce an exciting series of arcades, which add to the interest of this imaginative school and community facility.

188

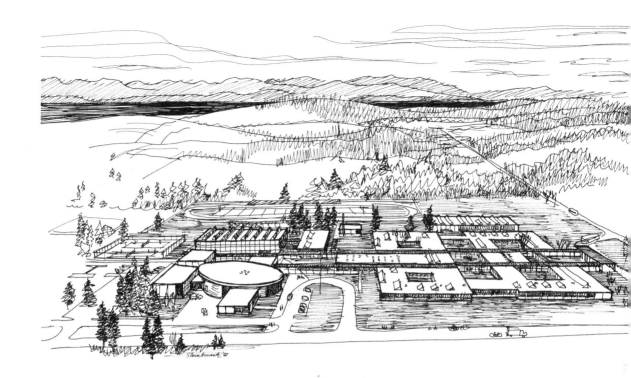

At 7608 212th Avenue Southwest in Edmonds is the complete educational and community facility of the Edmonds Senior High School. The buildings occupy seven acres on a total site of thirty acres which includes a complete and outstanding athletic plant for general student use as well as for interscholastic and community activities. Twelve hundred students are accommodated by fifty-six teaching stations, which, with other related facilities, are grouped into a campus plan. There are also a "cafetorium," little theater, and student social center in this steel frame building, which has an exterior of precast exposed aggregate panels. A large gymnasium is noteworthy because of its natural lighting, which is obtained through the A-frame trussed roof structure. Landscaped courts, sculptural in form, separate the various wings. This impressive project is used by the entire community for many activities, including continuing education. It was built in 1958 by architects Waldron and Dietz, with Dan Miller, associate.

Acknowledgments

Thanks are gratefully tendered to the following: the architects who created the buildings and who gave necessary information; the Seattle Chapter of the American Institute of Architects and its officers and members for their encouragement and support; Philip W. Bailey, publisher and editor, for allowing sketches to be used which have previously appeared in the *Argus*; the Museum of History and Industry and its governing organization, the Seattle Historical Society, for allowing material in their collection to be used or copied freely, and Mrs. Sutton Gustison, director, and Mrs. George W. Corley, Jr., curator; the University of Washington Press staff and especially William James, production manager, Naomi B. Pascal, editor, and Dianne Weiss, production assistant; the University of Washington College of Architecture and Urban Planning faculty and staff and especially Professor Myer R. Wolfe of the faculty, and Isabelle H. Reynolds, Judile Dare, and Leslie J. Morse of the secretarial staff, and Betty L. Austin, librarian; architects, planners, and critics of the city scene, including Kevin Lynch, Sydney H. William, Lewis Mumford, Stephen W. Jacobs, Barclay G. Jones, and Catherine Bauer Wurster, and philosopher Bertram E. Jessup, whose studies and writings have influenced this work unbeknownst to them; my wife, Elaine, for encouragement, patience, and understanding, and our children, Matthew, Lisa, David, and Peter, for happily accompanying me at times while sketching.

An earlier work of mine, *A Guide to Seattle Architecture 1850–1953* (New York: Reinhold Publishing Corp., 1953), has provided background and reference material.

Wherever possible, existing subjects were sketched on location. A Rapidograph pen or a fountain pen was used.

Particular attention is called to the fact that the privacy of owners of homes should be respected. Since the homes are not open to visitors, it is suggested that anyone who wishes to visit a house should contact the architect, who may, if possible, arrange a visit.

VICTOR STEINBRUECK, A.I.A.

February, 1962
Seattle

List of Buildings and Places